Sabbath Born

"**Thriving on the love of God** with a great generosity of spirit is the theme of Skarda's heartwarming essays. He conveys the wisdom that comes from viewing each day as a gift to grow our spiritual nature so we blossom as ambassadors of God's love."

—**Regina V. Cates,** creator of *Romancing Your Soul,* and author of the bestselling book *Lead with Your Heart, Creating a Life of Love Compassion and Purpose*

"*Sabbath Born* **is an inspiring collection** of scripture based personal stories and is a reservoir for bible studies and book clubs. This is Britt Skarda's first book and I hope it won't be his last."

—**James L. "Skip" Rutherford III,** Dean Emeritus University of Arkansas Clinton School of Public Service

Sabbath Born

Reflections of a Reluctant Prophet

Britt Allen Skarda

Parkhurst Brothers Publishers
MARION, MICHIGAN

www.parkhurstbrothers.com

Consumers may order Parkhurst Brothers books from their favorite online or bricks-and-mortar booksellers, expecting prompt delivery. Parkhurst Brothers books are distributed to the trade through the Chicago Distribution Center. Trade and library orders may be placed through Ingram Book Company, Baker & Taylor, Follett Library Resources, and other book industry wholesalers. To order from Chicago Distribution Center, phone 1-800-621-2736 or fax to 800-621-8476. Copies of this and other Parkhurst Brothers Publishers titles are available to organizations and corporations for purchase in quantity by contacting the Special Sales Department at our home office location, listed on our website. Manuscript submission guidelines for this publishing company are available at our website.

Printed in the United States of America

First Edition, November 2022

Printing history: 2022 2023 2024 2025 8 7 6 5 4 3 2 1

Library Cataloging Data Author–Skarda, Britt A., American Christian storyteller and author
  1.   Subject–Christianity, Americana
  2.   Subject–Spirituality/Christian
  2020-trade paperback and e-book

ISBN: Trade Paperback   978-1-62491-191-0
ISBN: e-book   978-1-62491-192-7

Cover and interior design by   Linda D. Parkhurst, PhD
Acquired for Parkhurst Brothers Publishers and edited by   Ted Parkhurst
Proofreading by   T. Percival Layman
Cover Photo Credit: ID 115177001 © Artjuli933 | Dreamstime.com

112022

This book is dedicated to

Karen

who has made the journey with me through forty-nine years

of sabbaths and every day in between.

Acknowledgments

Over the course of my life, I have been blessed to stand on the shoulders of giants who shaped and inspired me to take fearless strides that I would otherwise never have attempted. One of these audacious steps has been the composition of this book. While it would be impossible to name all of them, let me take my best shot at shouting out the names of some of these remarkable people.

First, for my wife, Karen, who has listened, encouraged, and loved me for a half-century now, oftentimes to the neglect of allowing her own extraordinary talents to shine forth. This work would not have come to fruition without you. For my children, children-in-love, and grandchildren: Natalie and Brent, Brittany and Nick, Peter and Chancey, Luke, Levi, Jackson and Vivian. Your love and your lives have inspired me and helped me to fulfill the greatest calling of my life—to become Dad and Daddo. Thank you! For my late parents, Joe and Cannie Skarda, who conceived and brought me into this world, named me, and imprinted my soul with the values I hold dear to this very day. You may not have been heavy-duty church-goers, but your passion for selflessly giving back to the community and those in need served as an outward and visible sign of an inward and spiritual grace.

My deep appreciation to Parkhurst Brothers Publishers, especially Ted Parkhurst, who encouraged me to write this book ten years ago (I finally listened, Ted!). For the late Dr. Gerald M. Schumann, who delivered me on a Sunday morning almost seven decades ago, thanks for being "on-call" to help this nine-pound,fourteen-ounce baby boy land safely.

For my grandparents and great grandparents: Natalie, Claron, Frances, Ruth, and Nat. Though you have been gone from both this world and my sight for decades now, I can still feel your presence and hear your voices encouraging me to strive for remarkable things I could only imagine as a child. For my extended family members: siblings, aunts, uncles, cousins, in-laws and outlaws, your presence and participation in my life has greatly contributed to this work.

For the churches I served over a period of thirty-five years: Banks/Grove Hill United Methodist Churches, Wilton, NC; Brookston Presbyterian Church, Henderson, NC; Bearden/Thornton United Methodist Churches, Bearden, AR; Henderson United Methodist Church, Little Rock, AR; First United Methodist Church, Springdale, AR; and Pulaski Heights United Methodist Church, Little Rock, AR. Thank you for the life lessons I learned from you. For the thousands of parishioners who graciously claimed me as your pastor over the years, you will never know how much it meant to baptize, confirm, marry, bury and pray for you and your loved ones. It was a sacred trust I never took lightly.

Last, but certainly not least, thanks be to God!

Contents

The Birth of Reluctance

Monday's child is fair of face,
Tuesday's child is full of grace.
Wednesday's child is full of woe,
Thursday's child has far to go.
Friday's child is loving and giving,
Saturday's child works hard for a living.
And the child born on the Sabbath day
Is bonny and blithe, good and gay.[1]

IF THE OLD FORTUNE-TELLING SONG "Monday's Child," which ostensibly foretells a child's character based on the day of his or her birth, is true, then I was destined to live my life as a happy-go-lucky person. "And the child born on the Sabbath day is bonny and blithe, good and gay." That's the way the song puts it, and at least in my case, it appears to be so. I am a happy individual with a can-do attitude and a positive outlook on

---

1. Although the oral tradition of this nursery rhyme goes back to 1570, it was first recorded in Mrs. A.E. *Bray's Traditions, Superstitions, and Sketches of Devonshire,* Vol 2. in 1838.

life. However, there is also another dimension to my personality. Apparently, I was destined to become, not only a cheerful person, but a person of faith as well.

Born January 31, 1954, I made my inaugural appearance in the delivery room of a small-town hospital housed inside a converted storefront building that had previously served as my great grandfather's mercantile store. The doctor who delivered me was a native of the Bronx, New York. An army surgeon during World War II, he relocated to rural Des Arc, Arkansas, following the war after responding to a recruitment ad in a medical journal.

A convert from Judaism to Christianity, the good doctor made it a practice of gifting every new baby he delivered with a copy of the Good Book. The inscription inside my first Bible stamped "Des Arc General Hospital" reads, *"Property of Master Britt Allen Skarda since Sunday, 8:20 AM, January 31, 1954."* In keeping with this auspicious spiritual beginning, my parents carried me down the aisle of the local Methodist Church, where I was baptized at the tender age of three months by a pastor named Wesley. However, this is where my religious connections began to wane.

I was raised in a nominally Christian home. My parents were not churchgoers, so I spent Sunday mornings in front of the TV watching programs like *The Big Picture* and *Bullwinkle*. As a matter of fact, much of my early religious instruction came from the clay-animated TV series *Davey and Goliath*, produced by the Lutheran Church in America. To this day,

I am reminded of *Davey and Goliath* whenever I sing the majestic hymn *A Mighty Fortress is Our God,* which served as the show's theme music.

My three brothers and I did manage to attend Sunday school sporadically. Our mom would drop us off at the front of the church and return an hour later to retrieve us. I rarely attended worship as a child, though I recall one magical experience of sitting with my maternal grandmother in the sanctuary on Sunday morning. When it came time to go forward for Holy Communion, Nannie had me wait in the pew while she received the elements.

I was fourteen years old before I returned to worship again. On that day, I received my first-ever Holy Communion. I was disappointed to find the elements consisted of tiny shot glasses filled with grape juice accompanied by crumbled saltine crackers on a silver tray. I remember telling myself that this version of the sacrament felt more like a child's tea party than the supper of the Lord.

I never doubted God for a single moment, nor experienced any serious crises of faith during my formative years—I always believed. However, my faith didn't readily fit into the confines of organized religion. I was never confirmed as a youth. Neither did I attend summer church camp or participate in my local congregation's Sunday evening youth group. Due to my family's lack of hands-on involvement with the church, I felt like an outsider. I had no idea what a potluck supper was all about, and being "saved" sounded to me like the successful result of a search and rescue mission.

At the tender age of ten, I tried bridging the gap of separation between the institutional church and me by participating in the annual children's Christmas pageant. I memorized my part and performed it to perfection before a large Sunday evening crowd. I was ecstatic! The pageant ended with a visit from Santa Claus, who burst through the front doors of the sanctuary and bellowed "Ho! Ho! Ho!" as he made his way down the center aisle to the chancel. After Santa took a seat on his throne next to the Christmas tree, we children pressed forward to receive our gifts of apples and oranges tied up in brown paper bags.

In the flurry of activity, I accidentally bumped into a little girl standing next to me. Immediately, I heard the angry voice of the child's mother growling at me, "Watch where you're stepping!" I looked up to see the face of a monster dressed in taffeta giving me the stink eye. Emotionally destroyed, I left the church determined never to return.

Yes, I went back, but years later I had a similar experience as a high school student. I was sitting in a pew with my girlfriend one Sunday morning, and we were innocently giggling and whispering in each other's ears, when suddenly a mink-clad matron seated in front of us turned around, and with a look that could kill, screamed, "Sinful! Just sinful!" I don't remember anything else about worship that day except that I sprang out of there as soon as the benediction was offered.

My reluctance to embrace organized religion continued

to grow. As a high school student, I joined an interdenomina-
tional choir that the largest church in town sponsored. I thoroughly enjoyed the camaraderie that was engendered through
singing songs of praise together. Alas, one day at the end of
choir practice, I was hustled off to an isolated room by the
choir director and a couple of fellow choir members from the
host church. They politely told me that they were concerned
about my salvation. They instructed me to pray the sinners'
prayer and accept Jesus Christ as my personal Lord and Savior.
I complied. However, when they told me I needed to recant my
wishy-washy baptism as an infant by being plunged beneath
the saving waters of their fiberglass baptistry, I bolted and ran.

During the "Jesus movement" of the late sixties and early
seventies, I was invited to join a group that met weekly in
homes to study the Bible and share prayer concerns. Reluctantly, I attended one of these sessions. Not so surprisingly,
my first visit ended badly when the leader offered a prayer of
thanksgiving to God for leading yet another lost soul into their
midst. I left the group, never to return.

I cannot begin to list the instances in my early years in
which I was left feeling spiritually damaged by the good inten-
tions of virtuous Christian people. Don't get me wrong. I've
never had a problem with Jesus. Like the Doobie Brothers, I
affirm that "Jesus is just alright with me, Jesus is just alright, oh
yeah!" And yet, like Gandhi, who famously said, "I like your
Christ, I do not like your Christians. Your Christians are so
unlike your Christ," I struggled with Christ's body, the church.

So, what happened along the way that led me into a thirty-three-year career serving churches as a United Methodist pastor? Was I, like the prophet Isaiah, awestruck by the presence of God's holiness as I entered the temple one day? Was I, like Paul, struck blind by the appearance of the resurrected Christ on the road to Damascus?

Actually, the answer is a simple four-letter word: L-O-V-E. From marriage, to parenthood, to friendships, to the death of family members, I found myself thriving on the love of God. For me, love became the benchmark for every decision and action in my personal life and my professional life. Love led me to forgive the hurtful actions and bad theology of fellow believers that had driven me away from the church for so many years.

A significant portion of my calling these past three decades has been focused on dispelling the myth of an angry, vengeful and judgmental God by illuminating the one true God—the God revealed to us in Jesus Christ. May the reflections found within this book inspire you to seek your better angels.

Soli Deo Gloria!

Shouting Stones

BASED ON LUKE 19: 29-40

The river was cut by the world's great flood and runs over rocks from the basement of time. On some of the rocks are timeless raindrops. Under the rocks are the words, and some of the words are theirs.... [2]

Some of the Pharisees in the crowd said to him, "Teacher, order your disciples to stop," and Jesus answered,
"I tell you, if these were silent, the stones would shout out...." [3]

FROM THE WORDS OF AMERICAN AUTHOR NORMAN MACLEAN in *A River Runs Through It* to the words of Jesus in the gospel according to Luke, we are reminded that stones have served as a powerful witness since time immemorial. From the massive stones that comprise the ancient pyramids of Egypt to the stones that form the Temple Mount in Jerusalem—from the Moai, those monolithic Easter Island stones carved in the likeness of human faces to the original "little rock" that gave birth

---

2   Norman Maclean, *A River Runs Through It, and Other Stories,* First Edition, Chicago: University of Chicago Press, 1976
3   Luke 19: 39-40

to the name of Arkansas' Capitol City, stones speak to us of other times, places, people, and events. Stones speak to us of eternity—they speak to us of God.

Perhaps you have your own personal stones that bear witness to your life. I do. I have a native American stone I plucked from a creek bed on our family farm more than sixty years ago. It was once used by an ancient civilization to grind maize; it speaks of a civilization that disappeared more than a thousand years ago. I also have two large stones positioned beneath an oak tree in my backyard, where I sit and tell stories to my grandchildren. And then there is the sill outside our kitchen window loaded with stones my grandchildren have collected from our yard.

These stones are sacred to me, and I look forward to the end of the COVID pandemic when my family can come together again to tell more stories and collect more stones. Novelist Maclean said it best: "Under the rocks are the words, and some of the words are theirs."

The Bible is filled with stories of stones that have borne witness to God's power and love down through the ages. In the book of Genesis, Jacob rests his head upon a stone at a place called *Bethel*, which means the house of God. In Exodus, Moses ascends Mt. Sinai to receive God's law that has been etched into stone tablets. In First Samuel, David hurls a stone at the giant Goliath in an effort to protect God's people from harm. In John's gospel, an angry crowd is poised to hurl stones at a woman caught in adultery until Jesus warns them, "No!

Not unless you are without sin yourself." In the book of Acts, Stephen, the first Christian martyr, is executed with a hailstorm of stones, even as he prays forgiveness for his executioners. And then there are these stones we find in the nineteenth chapter of Luke's gospel:

> *As he was now approaching the path down from the Mount of Olives, the whole multitude of the disciples began to praise God joyfully with a loud voice for all the deeds of power that they had seen, saying, "Blessed is the king who comes in the name of the Lord! Peace in heaven, and glory in the highest heaven!"*
>
> *Some of the Pharisees in the crowd said to Jesus, "Teacher, order your disciples to stop."*
>
> *He answered, "I tell you, if these were silent, the stones would shout out."*[4]

Shouting stones! What are these stones that Jesus speaks of anyway, and what do they have to shout about? Something important, no doubt, since this story of Jesus' entry into Jerusalem is recorded by all four gospel writers, Matthew, Mark, Luke, and John. Think about it. Only two gospel writers record the story of Jesus' birth—only two record the Lord's Prayer, the prayer he taught his disciples—and only one gospel writer records Jesus' most iconic parables, the parable of the good Samaritan and the parable of the prodigal son. There must be something critically important about this particular story.

---

4   Luke 19: 37-40

As Jesus descends from the Mount of Olives on the back of a donkey, Luke tells us that a whole multitude of disciples began praising their new king. A whole multitude? An entire multitude must surely mean more than just Jesus' twelve disciples, right? It must mean others, many others, but who? Who makes up this vast throng that throws their cloaks on the ground before Jesus?

How about Zacchaeus, the tax collector whose life was transformed by an encounter with the Lord? Or perhaps Jairus and his young daughter, whom Jesus raised from the dead? Maybe the lepers he healed are present, including those who failed to return to thank him for their healing? It's almost certain the women, Mary Magdalene, Joanna, and Mary, the mother of James, who would remain at his side until the bitter end, were there? And I have no doubt the woman at the well who discovered in Jesus "the Living Water that never runs dry"[5] was present that fateful day. The possibilities are endless.

Jesus' entry into Jerusalem is remarkable because, until this very moment, his followers have been just that, followers— quiet and passive. When Jesus called out the civil and religious authorities of his day for their injustices, his followers grew tense but said nothing in Jesus' defense. When Jesus defended a prostitute, they blushed and looked the other way. When he made the startling announcement that "the last shall be first and the first shall be last,"[6] they were secretly overjoyed but kept a poker face.

---

5   Lailah Gifty Akita, an inspirational writer from Accra, Ghana.
6   Matthew 20:16

But not today! Today, as Jesus enters Jerusalem, every shred of doubt has been erased. There is no more reluctance—no more fear—no more silence. Instead, the crowd boldly shouts to the heavens, "Blessed is he who comes in the name of the Lord! Hosanna in the highest!"[7] Yes, this adoration will be short-lived. We know what happens to Jesus later this same week. Shouts of *Hosanna* will be replaced with cries of *Crucify him!* And this is where the shouting stones come in: "I tell you, if these are silent, the stones will shout out!"[8] Jesus proclaims to us that you and I are those shouting stones. We are called to be those living, breathing, shouting stones for the world.

You and I were created to bear witness to God's love in Jesus Christ. In the midst of sorrow and sadness, in the midst of tragedy, in the midst of this horrible global pandemic, we can serve as shouting stones. We can shout out! We can shout out by proclaiming the good news that *God is with us! God is with us! God is with us!*

Like your neighborhood, my neighborhood feels different these days. Homes are shuttered, and people are distancing themselves from one another. When we walk in our neighborhood, we cross to the other side of the street to avoid close contact with our neighbors lest we become infected with COVID-19. However, this past week several children in the neighborhood did something remarkable. They gathered up random stones, painted them purple and gold, added glitter,

---

7   Matthew 21:9
8   Luke 19:40

and left one at the curb of each and every home in the neighborhood as a sign of hope.

I tell you, if these were silent, the stones would shout out!

Under the rocks are the words, and some of the words are theirs.

⌒

Last is First

BASED ON LUKE 1:68-79

"A BABY IS GOD'S OPINION THAT LIFE SHOULD GO ON,"[9] wrote poet Carl Sandburg and I couldn't agree more. Karen and I even had Sandburg's quote engraved on our first child's birth announcement. Is there anything more hopeful or healing than holding a baby in our arms? Babies have the power to calm us—slow our heart rate and breathing level until it takes on the steady rhythm of a cat's purr. One of the best perks I receive as a pastor is holding and baptizing infants as these brand-new human beings begin the journey of faith with their families. For me, this joy has only been exceeded by being a father and grandfather and holding my own babies.

I do confess, however, that as a parent and grandparent, I'm a second-class citizen. I am! I can't begin to compete with Karen. She has always been Johnny-on-the-spot for all of the babies in our family by loving, rocking, feeding, and nurturing them. Karen doesn't mind changing dirty diapers or cleaning smelly spit-up. I do. As a result, in times of need, our children and grandchildren have been conditioned to turn to Karen

---

9   Carl Sandburg, Remembrance Rock, New York, NY, Harcourt Brace Hovanovich, Inc., 1948

first and me second. I understand! I know my place! Karen is Queen Elizabeth, ruler of the United Kingdom, and I'm Philip, Duke of Edinburgh. I stand in her shadow.

It's not that I haven't fantasized or even tried to over-throw my wife's exalted position. I have. In preparation for the birth of our firstborn, Natalie, I spent six weeks in Lamaze classes learning how to coach Karen through childbirth. However, when we got into the delivery room, and Karen's labor pains became intense, I realized I was out of my league. This was all about her. The same is true of our second child, Brittany. I thought it was pretty special when our daughter made her grand entrance on Christmas morning, that is until I found myself alone in the hospital cafeteria eating Jello® while "Madonna" and child bonded in the nursery upstairs.

Third time's a charm, as they say, so I knew I had dethroned Karen when the long-awaited phone call came from the adop-tion agency in Washington, D.C., telling us that we had a new infant son, Peter, who had been born in Seoul, Korea. Because I took the call, I had the privilege of sitting Karen down and telling her the good news, "Guess what, honey? We're going to have a boy!" But it didn't take long following his arrival for Karen to win our son's heart, and my position was again rele-gated to last place.

Truth be told, I've spent most of my parenting and grandparenting years playing Joseph to Karen's Virgin Mary. Yes, I'm Joseph, that enigmatic behind-the-scenes figure who never speaks a word, not a single solitary word in the gospels, as opposed to Mary, the mother of Jesus, who belts out her powerful and moving Magnificat loud and clear: "My soul magnifies the Lord, and my spirit rejoices in God my Savior!"[10] And, yes, I am ok with my position because I've learned that life is not so much about holding the first-place position as it is about simply having a part, even if that role is last place.

I love Mary, and I love her song. We will eventually get to her later in the holy season of Advent. However, today we listen to the song of a lesser-known figure—Zechariah—and his words are also powerful.

> *Blessed be the Lord God of Israel, for he has looked favorably on his people and redeemed them. He has raised up a mighty Savior for us in the house of his servant David, as he spoke through the mouth of his holy prophets from of old, that we would be saved from our enemies and from the hand of all who hate us.[11]*

For those of you who are not familiar with him, Zechariah is a priest, and his wife Elizabeth is Mary's cousin. The couple has never been able to conceive children, and now they are old like Abraham and Sarah of Old Testament fame. They have given up any hope of becoming parents. But one day, as Zechariah enters the holy of holies to light the sacred incense, the angel Gabriel appears and tells him that he and Elizabeth will have a son, and they will name him John. Zechariah pushes back and gives Gabriel some lip—tells the angel

---

10   Luke 1:46-55
11   Luke 1: 68-71

there is no way he and Elizabeth will ever have a baby at their advanced age.

It's not good to smart-mouth God. Gabriel shuts Zechariah's mouth with a case of laryngitis that is so severe it hangs on for the next nine months. All Zechariah can do is scribble notes and watch and wonder as Elizabeth's belly grows bigger and bigger, even as his eyes grow rounder and rounder. Eventually, Elizabeth delivers a son. After eight days, she and Zechariah take the child to the temple to be circumcised according to Jewish custom. When Zechariah is asked, "What name is given this child?" he writes it down on a piece of paper because he cannot speak, but suddenly his mouth is miraculously opened, and he cries, "John! John! His name is John!"[12]

The old priest doesn't stop here. He continues. He praises God by giving thanks for the coming Messiah, Jesus, the one who will fulfill Israel's fondest hopes and dreams—the one who is the Alpha and Omega—the Beginning and the End—the First and the Last. Finally, he concludes by offering a special blessing for his own son, John:

> And you, child, will be called the prophet of the Most High; for you will go before the Lord to prepare his ways, to give knowledge of salvation to his people by the forgiveness of their sins. By the tender mercy of our God, the dawn from on high will break upon us, "To give light to those who sit in darkness and in the shadow of death, to guide our feet into the way of peace."[13]

---

12 Luke 1:63
13 Luke 1: 76-79

And sure enough, later in Luke's gospel, we find John all grown up, emerging from the wilderness. He baptizes throngs of people with water even as he proclaims the coming of the One who will baptize with fire and the Holy Spirit. John may not be first, but he's certainly not last! His contribution is powerful!

In the parable of the wedding feast that depicts dinner guests scrambling for the most prominent seats at the head of the table, Jesus advises his listeners to take the last seat at the table instead. In doing so, they somehow find themselves in a place of honor. Likewise, Jesus ends his parable of the workers in the vineyard with the statement, "The last will be first, and the first will be last."[14]

I've been doing a lot of thinking this Advent season about the state of the world: the steady destruction of the environment—the growing gun violence in our nation—a Congress that refuses to address the fact that we're killing ourselves from within—arrogant political candidates who invoke God's name but offer none of God's love—not to mention our collective arrogance that always seems to put ourselves first. I've been thinking this Advent season that instead of lighting candles, singing Christmas carols, and making merry, we should dress in sackcloth and ashes. We should get down on our knees, wash our neighbor's feet, beat swords into plowshares, and put ourselves last, just like the child whose birth we gather to celebrate.

⌣

14   Luke 13:30

An Empty Chair

BASED ON MATTHEW 25: 31-46

MY PATERNAL GRANDMOTHER had already reached her seventieth birthday by the time I was born. Because she was well-advanced in years, I did not have the opportunity to spend extended periods of time with her when I was growing up. As a matter of fact, most of my contact with my grandmother was limited to Sunday afternoon visits with my parents.

Grandmother had been born in Iowa, but she was thoroughly "Old World" in outlook and appearance. Her parents had immigrated to the United States from Bohemia in the 1870s. As a result, she was steeped in the culture of her family's homeland. My grandmother was a pleasant, round-faced woman with a short, stocky build. She wore filmy, spiderweb hairnets, long dresses, sensible black shoes, and stockings that sagged at the ankles. Grandmother was an enigmatic figure in my life.

One thing about my grandmother that was not mysterious at all was her gift for hospitality. Whenever my parents dragged my brothers and me to Grandmother's house for a Sunday afternoon visit, we would find her standing in the doorway as though she had been waiting for us all day. After embracing each grandson, Grandmother would invite us to sit around the kitchen table. Thus, She would begin the ritual of passing out treats. First came the pressed glass candy dish filled with peppermints. "Go ahead! Take more!" Grandmother would insist when I selected a single piece of candy. Next, she would pass around a tray of freshly baked Kolaches, a Bohemian sweet bread filled with stewed prunes. They smelled like heaven.

Finally, if we were lucky, the table ritual would end with tiny glasses of red wine for each of us. My temperance-minded Methodist mother was shocked at this offering, but she never protested. After all, this was Grandmother's table, and she was the high priestess when we were guests in her temple.

Forty years later, whenever I recall my grandmother's life, the image that comes immediately to mind is an empty kitchen chair. Because Grandmother was always in the process of serving others, she never had time to sit down at the table herself. One chair was left empty.

In the American south, there is an old tradition of leaving an empty chair at the table during mealtime. This chair serves as a visible reminder that, no matter how many are present at the table, there is always room for one more. Another place can be set, and another glass of wine can be poured.

In Matthew's gospel, we find one of the most disturbing stories ever told in scripture, and it comes from the mouth of Jesus himself. It is the account of the last judgment. "When the Son of Man comes in his glory … then he will sit on his throne ... and he will separate them one from another as a shepherd separates the sheep from the goats."[15] What's so disturbing about this particular story? To be perfectly honest, it's Jesus' criteria for getting into heaven that I find unsettling.

If we compare Jesus' guidelines to ours today, we soon discover that he doesn't ask the sheep the standard "salvation questions" we use in the church today. Jesus doesn't ask them if they have prayed the sinner's prayer, if they have accepted him as Lord and Savior, or even if they have been baptized. Jesus simply says, "I was hungry, thirsty, sick, naked, a stranger and in prison, and you pulled up an empty chair and welcomed me at your table."[16] It seems Jesus' criteria for entering the kingdom isn't so much about what we say as it is about how we show hospitality to those in need.

By providing an empty chair for people who previously have not had a place at the table, we live out the essence of Christ's message to a hurting world. We offer the promise of salvation to others. Thank you, Grandmother, for a lesson in kingdom-building!

⌣

15 Matthew 25:31-33
16 Matthew 25:34-46

How To Bury A Dog

MY DOG DIED. IT WAS NO BIG DEAL, or so I thought. Karen and I adopted Jazz the summer we married. We were college undergrads, and he was the first addition to our newly-formed family. We found him on a weekend trip to northwest Arkansas. Advertised as a purebred registered Cocker Spaniel, he turned out to be pure Heinz 57 instead. From the beginning, he was bad news. It took forever to housebreak him, and he chewed up everything in sight: the carpeting, the furniture, our shoes, Karen's handmade macrame plant holders, and my Steely Dan album collection.

To make matters worse, within weeks after bringing him home, he was diagnosed with a seizure disorder. It cost us a small fortune to keep him in meds. I don't know how else to express it: I hated that dog, but I also loved that dog. His life was miserable, and he made my life miserable. The misery Jazz introduced into our lives was strangely meaningful. Our co-dependent relationship lasted four long years.

And then one night, without warning, he died during a massive seizure. I should've felt relief that the long nightmare had finally come to an end, but I didn't. Instead, as I gazed down at his lifeless form, grief swept over me. I gathered him up in my arms, cradled his little body, and wept like I'd never wept before. Here I was, a grown man with a wife, a college degree, a career, a six-month-old child, a home, and a mortgage, and I wept like a baby. It didn't make sense. I had just buried my father, who died without warning only one month earlier. I had been a pillar of strength throughout the family's sad ordeal. I had supported my mom and other family members. I had even helped make my father's funeral arrangements, including selecting the casket and grave marker. I had managed to maintain a poker face throughout the process. Now, here I was sobbing over a dead dog.

I sat up all night in the laundry room with Jazz's body. I wrapped him in a blanket the next day and buried him beneath a redbud tree in the backyard. I placed all of Jazz's worldly possessions in his open grave: his rubber bone, rawhide chew toy, and the tattered towel he dragged around like Linus' blanket, and I covered it with dirt. And then I sat down and cried some more.

Several weeks passed, and I found myself telling my pastor the story of how I had buried my dog. I spoke of the overwhelming grief I had felt, accompanied by a flood of tears. I told him I didn't understand why I had been so devastated, especially after sailing through my dad's death relatively unscathed just weeks earlier. He looked me in the eye and spoke matter-of-factly, "God killed your dog." "What?!" I responded. This occurred several years prior to my own call to ordained ministry, so my theological knowledge at this point was minimal.

"What?!" I asked again.

"God killed your dog," he responded, "so that you could grieve the death of your father." I thought about it for a moment, and I understood. He was right.

No, I don't believe God is in the business of killing little dogs or any other creature, for that matter. God doesn't send tornadoes, floods, or hurricanes to punish or teach us a lesson. God doesn't take the people we love away from us. God is love, plain and simple. But God has an amazing ability to use the broken places in our lives to bring about wholeness. In my case, the death of my dog served as a catalyst to help me fully grieve the loss of my dad.

Some of the most gut-wrenching experiences in our lives can lead to some of our most healing experiences. Moments of sadness prompt flashes of joy. Moments of grief open avenues of faith that we never dreamed possible. Disappointments and failures inspire us to set new goals and begin life anew. The apostle Paul summed it up beautifully in Romans 8:28, "We know that all things work together for good for those who love God, who are called according to God's purpose."

Think about those physical places in our nation today that commemorate death and suffering while also facilitating healing and hope: the National Vietnam Veterans' Memorial in Washington, DC, the National Holocaust Museum, and the 911 Memorial in New York City. These and others have the power to touch our hearts and heal our souls. In John's gospel, we find a similar dynamic at work:

> *And just as Moses lifted up the serpent in the wilderness, so must the Son of Man be lifted up, that whoever believes in him may have eternal life. For God so loved the world that he gave his only son, so that everyone who believes in him may not perish but may have eternal life.*[17]

John's reference to the "serpent in the wilderness" comes from a story in the Old Testament book of Numbers. Moses has been leading the Israelites through the wilderness on their forty-year trek when the Israelite camp suddenly becomes infested with poisonous snakes. People are dying. Moses intercedes by praying to God for help, and God responds by instructing Moses to fashion a serpent from bronze. God then tells Moses to place the serpent on a standard in the midst of the Israelites, and whenever a member of the community is bitten, they need only to look upon the image of the bronze serpent to be healed.[18] The writer of John's gospel tells us that Jesus Christ is our bronze serpent, our Vietnam or 911 Memorial.

Through Jesus' suffering, death and resurrection, we find life and hope. Through the horror of the cross, we find healing for our souls. This is what distinguishes Christianity from other major world religions. Think about it. Most faiths are identified by symbols of light and beauty: The Star of David, The Crescent Moon, and the Lotus Blossom. Christianity is

---

17 John 3: 14-16
18   Numbers 21:6-9

different. Our symbol is one of suffering and pain, that of a naked and bloodied man nailed to a grotesque cross. Christianity asserts that, through Christ's suffering and death, we can find light and salvation if we will only look upon the cross and believe.

How does salvation work? I don't know. I can't explain it. It's a mystery. It comes to us by faith. All I know is that following Jesus has somehow changed my life for the better. Even as the death of my dog helped me to grieve and heal following the death of my father, so the death and resurrection of Jesus helps me die to self in order to find new purpose and meaning in life.

Thirty-six years have passed since I buried my dog. Macrame plant holders are passe today, and I left Steely Dan behind decades ago. And yet, from time to time, I still manage to resurrect that little dog in my heart and mind. He is there again with Karen and me as we work our way through college and our early years of marriage. He is there with us as we move into our first home. He is waiting at the front door as we bring our firstborn child home from the hospital. And he is with us as my father dies. Yep, I just keep resurrecting that little dog.

Do you know what I've learned? I've learned that it's hard to keep a good dog buried in a grave, and I've learned that it's also hard to keep a good savior buried in a tomb.

⟋⟋

A God of Disappointment

BASED ON JOB 42: 1-6

*What a piece of work is man, how noble in reason, how infinite
in faculties, in form and moving how express and admirable, in
action how like an angel, in apprehension how like a god: the
beauty of the world, the paragon of animals!*
—*William Shakespeare*

IT HAS BEEN TWENTY YEARS SINCE I FIRST HEARD these
immortal words from William Shakespeare's *Hamlet*, Act 2,
Scene 2, not in my high school literature class, but rather
while sitting in Little Rock's Robinson Auditorium watching
the Broadway musical *Hair*.

The raucous play had come to town amid a storm of
controversy surrounding its notorious nude scene. As an
impressionable teenager reading *Arkansas Gazette* editorials
protesting its premiere, my prurient interest got the best of
me, and I snuck off to see *Hair*. I piled into a car with a couple
of buddies, and we drove sixty-five miles down Interstate 40
through a dense fog to watch the controversial play.

I recall sitting in the darkened auditorium, eyes round as
saucers and mouth agape as the players sang, danced, cavorted

on stage, and openly struggled with sensitive issues of the day: drugs, sex, political corruption, pollution of the environment and the Vietnam War. The musical seemed to me to be a litany of the various ways in which the human race was slowly but surely killing itself.

Then, near the end, came the musical number with lyrics from Shakespeare's Hamlet: "What a piece of work is man, how noble in reason ..."[19] and, for me, there seemed to be great irony in these words. Until this moment, I had believed the human race was basically good. But, as I watched the ills of society paraded across the stage, I came to realize, for the first time in my life, that we are something less than perfect.

We really don't bear a very close resemblance to Shake-speare's lofty description of humanity. Our actions are not those of angels, and our apprehension is not that of a god. The psalmist sings out, "Thou hast made us little less than God."[20] Genesis claims that we are created "in the image of God,"[21] and even God, after creating us, says that we are "very good."[22] Yet, most of the time, we appear to be cheap imitations of what God intended us to be.

With our brokenness and addictions, the abuse we inflict upon one another, our fragmented families, our propensity for war, and our tendency to hate, we must surely ask ourselves: *Is God disappointed in us? Is God disappointed with the greatest*

19   Hamlet Act 2, Scene 2, 303–312
20   Psalm 8:5
21   Genesis 1:27
22   Genesis 1:31

creation, the paragon of animals? Rather than modeling Shakespeare's noble description of humanity, we more closely resemble the struggling, searching, fragmented, confused characters in the musical *Hair.*

Twenty years have passed since that night at Robinson Auditorium, and much has transpired in my life: marriage, children, a call to ordained ministry, a theological education, and, as a result, more questions. Now I struggle not only with the question of whether God is disappointed with us but with a more serious consideration: Is it possible that God has somehow not kept God's promises? Has The Redeemer not held up God's end of the bargain? Is it possible that the disappointments we sometimes face in our lives and in the world can be attributed at least in part to God?"

We know the definition of disappointment, don't we? Disappointment is when something falls short of our expectations. If we are honest, we must admit to moments when our relationship with God does indeed fall short of our expectations. For each of us, there comes a time when we feel as if God is ignoring us—refusing to hear our prayers. Who has not felt disappointment with God in the face of senseless tragedy? Who has not felt disappointment in the death of a child, a marriage, or a career?

Feelings of disappointment with God are timeless. The people of God have struggled with their disappointment since the beginning of time. Perhaps no one struggled more than Job. His story is intriguing.

One day Satan is strolling around heaven when he and God bump into each other. The two begin to make small talk which quickly turns to boasting. "Have you seen my man Job?" brags God to Satan, "There is none like him—best person in the entire world—no way your evil ways could ever infect him."

Satan quickly rebuts, "That's only because you've pampered him! You've given him everything a person could ever want: money, power, position, family, friends, health. Take it away, and he will curse you."

"Well, Satan, I'm not a gambling man," muses God, "But I'll make an exception this time. Go ahead. Do anything you want with Job. Repossess his farm. Infect his cattle with anthrax. Burn his home to the ground. Massacre his children. Destroy his health. Make him miserable. Do anything you want, but do not let him die. I'm willing to wager that Job will be faithful to the end." And so, with God's permission, Satan does exactly this. Satan takes everything from Job: his family, home, position, power, and health. Job is left sitting on the smoldering ashes of his life, scrapping the festering sores on his body with a potsherd and contemplating his feelings of disappointment with God.

Life is filled with disappointments. If we're honest with ourselves, there are times when, like Job, we feel as if God is somehow responsible for our difficulties. I was brought up to believe in a God who is involved in our lives—a deity who is intimately connected to God's people. God reached down to save the Israelites and led them into the promised land. God numbers the hairs on our heads. God listens and responds to our prayers. God cares.

But, if God cares enough to intervene, then God must also choose when not to intervene. If God steps in to save the passengers in the crash of a 747 jet, then God must also make the decision to refuse involvement when an automobile veers into an embankment, killing an entire family. A God so conflicted is sure to find his people disappointed.

Several weeks ago, I visited a longtime church member in the hospital. When I entered her room, the woman greeted me warmly with a kiss on the cheek. As we sat together, she told me she was looking forward to going home soon and eventually returning to church. She looked the picture of health. At the end of our visit, I offered a prayer that God would continue to bless her in the recovery process, and I left the hospital believing that all would be well.

The next morning, I received the news that the woman had died unexpectedly during the night. I immediately began to enumerate the many reasons this death was right. She would never again suffer or experience pain. She was now living in the presence of God in heaven. God needed her more than our church needed her. Suddenly I realized I sounded like Job's well-meaning friends, Bildad, Eliphaz, and Zophar, who offered all the conventional reasons for Job's suffering (sin, pride, refusal to repent, etc.), and I came to the realization that there was *no good reason* for this woman's death. She still had much to offer to her family, her church, and her community. The old, hackneyed excuses didn't work for me anymore. I was disappointed with God.

Disappointment with God is not a new experience for me. I've experienced it many times. I was disappointed with God when my young daughter's five-year-old playmate died a senseless death. I was disappointed with God when my father died suddenly and unexpectedly. I was disappointed with God when a young member of my congregation contracted the AIDS virus.

How do we handle our disappointment with God? How do we come to terms with a God who moves in mysterious ways? How do we justify a God who makes the sun rise, not only on the good, but on the evil as well? How do we embrace a God who allows the wicked to prosper while the good perish? How indeed? Perhaps the answer is to be found in Job's experience of God.

Job wrestled with feelings of pain and disappointment, and he struggled with God. But somehow, in the midst of the struggle (and even because of the struggle), Job had a living experience of God: "I had heard of thee by the hearing of the ear, but now my eye sees thee." [23] In the midst of his suffering, Job came to realize that a "relationship with God" is more important than life itself.

⌒

---

23   Job 42: 5

The woman lay dying in a hospital room. Every avenue of healing had been exhausted, but still, the disease continued to take its toll. Day by day, her friends from the church came and offered prayers for healing, yet the woman grew weaker and weaker. One day, as her friends were preparing to offer prayers for healing, the woman said to them, "Today, let's not pray that I'll be healed. God knows I hate this disease. Instead, let's pray that whatever happens, I'll be close to God because, in the end, this is what I really want."

Maybe the best thing we can say about our disappointment with God is that *God understands.* God understands what it means to be human; God became human in Jesus Christ. God understands what it means to suffer; God suffered death upon a cross. And God knows what it's like to feel disappointment; we disappoint God every day. But the good news is that God loves us despite our disappointing ways, and God still claims us as children of the divine. Can we do any less for God?

What a piece of work is man, how noble in reason, how infinite in faculties, in form and moving how express and admirable, in action how like an angel, in apprehension how like a god ...

Discover Your Birthright

Based on Ephesians 4: 1-16

As surely as the swallows return to Capistrano every spring, I return to the gulf coast every summer. I claim this annual pilgrimage to the beaches of Mississippi, Alabama, and the Florida panhandle as a personal birthright. My first-ever journey to the gulf coast dates back to the year 1959. I was only five years old, but I can still recall happily bouncing around in the back of the family station wagon with no seatbelts or air conditioning as my dad, cigarette in hand, steered us toward the beach with mom riding shotgun.

While I haven't been quite as faithful in my annual return to the beach as the swallows have been in their seasonal flight to Capistrano, I've only missed a handful of summers over the past sixty years. From childhood through puberty and beyond to adulthood, I've gravitated to the beach. I took Karen there when we were dating and only sixteen and nineteen years old. The beach would later become our honeymoon destination after we married. All of our children and grandchildren claim this birthright, as well.

But as wonderful and all-American as it may sound, there is a dark side to this beachy birthright because these annual jaunts into the deep south never fail to produce a certain level of anxiety within me. More often than not, I begin these journeys filled with fear. What if this happens? What if that happens? What if, God forbid, everything comes unglued along the way?

Some of my angst is justified. On that first journey back in 1959, my dad rear-ended a car while crossing the Mobile Bay Bridge as he stared out at the wreckage of a ship in the distance. Fortunately, no one was hurt, but it took a lot of duct tape and chicken wire to get the family car back to Arkansas in one piece. Over the years, there have been other mishaps: fender-benders, broken bones, jellyfish stings, a close encounter with a shark, and even a hurricane evacuation. Believe me! I look over my shoulder every time I go on vacation!

However, on our most recent trip to the beach, I learned a lesson in letting go of my fear. One bright morning as I was jogging along Perdido Beach Boulevard, another jogger began running toward me, waving her arms wildly and pointing over my left shoulder. *What's wrong?* I wondered. *Has some text-messaging teen lost control of his car? Has an 18-wheeler careened out of control? Am I about to be run over?*

In fear, I turned and looked over my shoulder just in time to see it—a rainbow—a magnificent rainbow in the sky! My fellow jogger had been directing my attention to a rainbow! My fears had been for naught!

Why would any believer embrace a birthright of fear when we have been blessed by a Creator who hangs rainbows in the sky to remind us of God's enduring love for us? "There is no fear in love, but perfect love casts out fear." [24] That's the way the writer of First John 4:18 puts it. This is our heritage! This is our birthright! Through the gift of God's love in Jesus Christ, we need not fear. We can overcome fender benders, jellyfish stings, and even shark bites because God is for us. And if God is for us, then who can be against us?

I don't know about you, but it seems to me that there is an awful lot of fear in the world today. We fear *too much* change. We fear *too little* change. We fear *this* group. We fear *that* group. And out of this fear, we have developed a nasty penchant for labeling, profiling, and denigrating others who are not like us. As much as I hate to admit it, a significant portion of this fear comes from those who profess to love and follow Jesus—those who call themselves Christian.

There is a "meanness" in many of our faith communities today, a kind of exclusivity that is the antithesis of the message Jesus taught. A blog post by writer John Pavlovitz, put it this way: "There's a bloated theology of fear, a [drumbeat] of perpetual impending doom that always comes in loud, spitting, screaming fury from pulpits and blog spots." [25] From issues related to immigration, to healthcare, to full rights for the LGBTQ+ community, the church, in far too many

---

24   1 John 4:18
25   John Pavlovitz, *Stuff That Needs To Be Said*, "Jurassic Church World: The Nearing Extinction of Dinosaur Christians," June 12, 2015, https://johnpavlovitz.com/2015/06/12/jurassic-church-world-the-nearing-extinction-of-dinosaur-christians/

instances, has pushed back and lashed out in hate.

This is why Paul's letter to the Ephesians, Chapter 4: 1-16, is so essential for the church today because Paul wrote these words from a prison cell to a world in which the social and religious landscape was changing rapidly:

> *I therefore, a prisoner in the Lord, beg you to lead a life*
> *worthy of the calling to which you have been called, with*
> *all humility and gentleness, with patience, bearing with one*
> *another in love, making every effort to maintain the unity*
> *of the Spirit in the bond of peace. There is one body and one*
> *Spirit, just as you were called to the one hope of your calling,*
> *one Lord, one faith, one baptism, one God and father of all,*
> *who is above all and through all and in all.*[26]

In his letter, Paul addressed a major theological shift taking place in the early church at the time, one that threatened the church's very existence. After thousands of years of being excluded from the faith—after being prohibited from entering the temple—after years of being scorned as unclean, unworthy, and uncircumcised—Gentiles had now been given full rights as members of the faith community. The doors of the church had been thrown wide open, and all were now welcome.

Do you understand what a radical change this was for the church? This was the early Christian version of the SCOTUS decision that affirmed same-gender marriage, only more so! This decision was explosive and potentially destructive because

---

26 Ephesians 4: 1-6

not everyone was on board with it. So, Paul, often labeled the "Apostle to the Gentiles," wrote this letter to the Ephesians as a call for unity. For Paul, unity was not the same as uniformity. We all know we are different from one another: We're male and female and black and white and gay and straight and young and old and Jew and Gentile. However, according to Paul, the traditional dividing wall has been imploded because Christ is with us. The world keeps spinning. The culture keeps shifting. Things keep right on changing. They always have, and always will, but now we can live together in unity.

Here's the deal. The only thing that remains the same in this world is Jesus Christ. Jesus is the same yesterday, today, and forever. Jesus is our non-negotiable. Jesus is our birthright. Do you know the oldest creed of the Christian church? Let me give you a hint. It dates to the first century, and it's not the Apostles' Creed or the Nicene Creed. These came along much later. No, the oldest creed of the church was simply this: "Jesus is Lord." Say it with me: "Jesus is Lord." Simple, isn't it? And Jesus calls us to keep it simple by loving everyone. This is our birthright.

Last week at the beach, I was watching TV with my five-year-old grandson Jackson when we began to play the old "I love you" game together. You know: "I love you so much! No! I love you more!" Finally, Jackson said, "Daddo, I love you, I love you, I love you! I can't even begin to describe how much I love you!" That's it! That's how much God loves us! And that's how much God loves those we don't love at all—those we feel are unworthy of God's love.

The night before we returned home from the beach, my grandson told his mom and dad he'd like to remain a kid and live at the beach forever. I think he was trying to say that sometimes we find ourselves in that perfect place where we look over our shoulder and see a rainbow behind us. In those moments, we know no fear, only perfect love.

Wouldn't it be wonderful if we Christians could recapture our birthright—a sense of perfect love—and carry it wherever we go?

⌐

Blackball

BASED ON LUKE 7: 36-50

Blackball: to vote against, reject, exclude.

THE ARCHAIC PRACTICE OF BLACKBALLING is alive and well today. It lives in business, education, sports, social circles, and even the church. Basically, to be blackballed is to be pushed out or not allowed into a particular circle or group. One can be blackballed in either formal or informal ways. Blackballing can be psychologically subtle, or it can be physically overt.

The term "blackball" derives from the ancient Greek practice of selecting members of a given group by placing either a black marble or a white marble in a box. When the voting is over, the box is opened. If all of the marbles are white, the individual is included in the group. However, if one or more marbles are black, the individual is excluded from the group.

Have you ever participated in a Greek-style blackball session complete with black and white marbles? I have. During my college days, forty years ago, I belonged to a fraternal organization. I loved my fraternity brothers, but we selected our new members via the blackball method, and I didn't love the prospect of exclusion. In late-night sessions, speaking in hushed tones behind locked doors, we would discuss the qualities of each prospective candidate before secretly dropping our black or white marbles in the box.

Most of the time, when the box was opened, it contained only white marbles, and our new brother was welcomed with open arms. But there were other times when an occasional blackball found its way into the box, indicating that someone had rejected the candidate. One rejected candidate had been a childhood friend of mine. He was younger than I, but we had grown up in the same small town and attended the same small church, so I knew him and his family. The discussion about my friend in the blackball session that night did not go well. It was harsh, even brutal. There was no way he was going to make the cut. Sure enough, he was blackballed that evening.

So, what had I personally done to help him out in this difficult situation? Nothing! I failed to speak up on his behalf. In fact, I remained silent throughout the entire blackball session. After all, I was a member in good standing. Why should I risk my place of privilege? My friend was devastated by the rejection. I was guilt-ridden. Fifteen years passed, and we lost touch with each other. And then, one day, he walked into my church office and told me he would like to become a member of my congregation. He said that he wanted to reconnect with the faith of his childhood. He told me that he was gay and that he was living with a full-blown case of AIDS. It was the height of the AIDS epidemic.

Now here's the redemptive part. In the fifteen years since that blackball session had left him feeling rejected, I had found my voice and my calling to serve Christ. "Of course, you're welcome!" I told him, "Jesus is not in the business of blackballing and excluding people. No! Jesus is in the business of loving and including people." My friend joined the church the following Sunday, and the congregation welcomed him with open arms. One year later, I held his hand as he lay in a hospital bed and died peacefully in his sleep. Days later, I preached his memorial service in the sanctuary of the church with a large gathering of those who were living with AIDS.

While I can't recall for sure the biblical text I used that day, I'm pretty sure this is it:

> *But you are a chosen race, a royal priesthood, a holy nation, God's own people, in order that you may proclaim the mighty acts of him who called you out of darkness into his marvelous light. Once you were no people, but now you're God's people; once you had not received mercy, but now you have received mercy.*[27]

For all the rhetoric we hear today from authoritarian religious figures insisting that God is an angry deity who is out to blackball us if we don't walk a very fine line, I disagree. Rather, I'm convinced that God loves every last one of us *unconditionally.* In the seventh chapter of Luke's Gospel, we find the biblical account of a blackball session with Jesus casting the deciding marble.

---

27   1 Peter 2:9-10

One of the Pharisees asked Jesus to eat with him, and he went into the Pharisee's house and took his place at the table. And a woman in the city, who was a sinner, having learned that he was eating in the Pharisee's house, brought an alabaster jar of ointment. She stood behind him at his feet, weeping, and began to bathe his feet with her tears and to dry them with her hair. Then she continued kissing his feet and anointing them with the ointment.[28]

Jesus, having been invited to Simon the Pharisee's home for dinner, is being entertained by one of the most influential religious figures in Jerusalem. The flow of the evening is interrupted when a woman, a notorious sinner and possibly even a prostitute, as indicated by her inappropriate display of affection, enters the room. She begins to weep and kiss Jesus' feet, bathe them with her tears, and dry them with her hair. She lavishes ointment on his feet and massages them.

Simon the Pharisee and the other dinner guests are put off, and rightly so. The woman's intimate act—bathing Jesus' feet and applying expensive oil—is unacceptable. In fact, it's downright pornographic! Women don't attend men's gatherings, and women don't touch men anywhere. Women don't let their hair down, not even with their husbands! By every measurable standard of decency, this woman should be stoned to death, and Jesus should be mortified. And, by the way, how does he know this woman? What must people be assuming about their relationship?

---

28 Luke 7: 36-38

Jesus needs to drop a blackball on her now or at least feign disgust in order to save face, but he doesn't. Instead, Jesus jumps to the woman's defense. He speaks up on her behalf. He confesses to the dinner guests that he knows her. He proclaims that this is a woman who the grace of God has saved. This woman has been forgiven, and she is expressing her appreciation in the only way she knows how; extravagantly and without regard for social convention.

Here is one who, rather than sitting quietly in Sunday morning worship following a rousing choral anthem, instead stands up, raises her hands in the air, and shouts to the astonishment of the rest of the congregation, "Praise the Lord! Thank you, Jesus! Thank you! Thank you!"

The difference between this woman and Simon the Pharisee is that she has been forgiven, and she knows it, while Simon doesn't even know that he needs forgiveness. Jesus tells him, "Simon, it's like the difference in being forgiven a debt of five dollars versus five hundred dollars. The more you are forgiven, the more you appreciate it. You must know that you are lost before you can be found." Sadly, Simon never seems to get it.

As my childhood friend lay dying of AIDS in a hospital bed, as the pounds continued to fall away and his skin began to hang from his frame like an ill-fitting bed sheet, he got it. He became more and more thankful every day. For him, the sky had never been so blue. The sunset had never been more dazzling. And the love and forgiveness of Jesus had never been more real.

Jesus never black-balled anyone, and neither should we.

⟶

Making God a Monster

BASED ON PSALM 103: 1-18

WHEN I WAS A BOY, going to bed at night triggered two predominant feelings within me, fear and comfort. Fear because, in my early years, I was obsessed with monsters. While I boldly stalked these creatures through the fields and forests surrounding my childhood home by day, at night, after my mom had tucked me into bed and turned out the light, I was terrified these fiends were lurking in my room. In an effort to stave off these intruders, I would pull the covers over my head and pray: *Now I lay me down to sleep. I pray the Lord my soul to keep....* And somehow, God showed up. My breathing slowed, I began to relax, and I felt comforted.

I know! I know! For those who are not believers, God is nothing more than a placebo, a way of making ourselves feel safe and secure. However, God has always been a real and present force in my life. I've never doubted God or God's love for me. While I eventually outgrew the monsters of my youth, I never outgrew God. God stuck with me and still does today. I don't know why. Perhaps my Methodist upbringing focused more on the Jesus who taught and healed and fed the hungry than on the God of vengeance who maimed, killed, and destroyed.

Of course, we all know there are real monsters in the world, don't we? Hurricanes and tsunamis swallow entire cities, pandemics decimate populations, corporations pollute our rivers to make a buck—and human monsters stalk and kill innocent victims. Make no mistake about it. There are monsters in the world, but the living God—the God of Abraham, Isaac, and Jacob—the God Jesus taught us to call "Abba, Father," Daddy, Mother Hen—is not one of them.

Karen and I have been married forty-five years now. We were mere children when we tied the knot. Three years into our marriage, at the ages of twenty-one and twenty-three, we welcomed our first child, a beautiful little girl. Five years into our marriage, we experienced a crisis of faith when our two-year-old daughter's three-year-old playmate and friend died suddenly and unexpectedly from meningitis. How do you tell your child that her friend is gone and she is never coming back? Where is God in a tragedy like this?

Karen and I attended the funeral held at a church, not of our particular tribe. I still recall sitting there in horror, squeezing Karen's hand as the pastor offered disturbing reason after disquieting reason for the death of this child. These platitudes ranged from: "God needed another angel" to accusing "the child's parents of having not been as active in church as they should have been, which may have influenced God's decision to take their child."

God was characterized as a monster who would kill a

child to make a point. By the time the service was over, I was undone. This experience was one of several that influenced my call to ordained ministry. "God deserves better than this," I told myself. "Is it possible I could become a convincing voice for the God of love?"

In his 2006 book *The God Delusion,* author and self-avowed atheist Richard Dawkins writes,

> The god of the Old Testament is arguably the most unpleasant character of all fiction: jealously proud of it; a petty, unjust, unforgiving control-freak; a vindictive, bloodthirsty, ethnic cleanser, a misogynistic, homophobic, racist, infanticidal, genocidal, pestilential, megalomaniacal, sadomasochistic, capriciously malevolent bully.

Phew! Harsh words, huh? But I can empathize with Hawkins' sentiment since there are numerous Old Testament texts from which these kinds of assumptions arise:

- In the Old Testament, sacrificing to any god other than Yahweh was a guaranteed death sentence.
- If a child became rebellious, God required the parents to stone their child to death.
- If a neighbor found another neighbor working on the sabbath, guess what? That neighbor was obliged to exterminate the working neighbor.
- And forget about engaging in premarital sex! Toast! Just toast!

Even the New Testament admonition from Paul found in Romans 13:1 that calls on the faithful "... to obey the governing authorities because they have been instituted by God ..." seems monstrous. Does this mean the faithful are called to obey the likes of Adolph Hitler? Saddam Hussein? Kim Jong-un? Vladimir Putin? Is this the God revealed to us in Jesus Christ, the Prince of Peace?

As a pastor, the theological question I am asked more often than any other is this: "Why does the God of the Old Testament seem so monstrous? So different from Jesus?" This incongruency is a stumbling block for would-be believers, not to mention happy fodder for budding atheists. As people of faith, how do we deal with the question of God as a monster? As I see it, there are three options:

- Option #1. We take the Bible at face value. We simply affirm that "God said it. I believe it. That settles it." This still leaves us with the question of what to do with a violent and monstrous God.

- Option #2. We can assert that "The Bible is not true at all—none of it—it's a collection of myths written by superstitious people thousands of years ago." This option leaves us with no God at all.

- Option #3. We can follow the example of Jesus.

The Old Testament was the only Bible Jesus ever knew, and he loved it. He lived by it, but he didn't endorse every word as coming directly from the mouth of God. "You have heard it said," Jesus would often say of a particular text, "But I say to you [this or that]." In his Sermon on the Mount, Jesus took one of the most monstrous statements ever attributed to

God from Deuteronomy, "an eye for an eye and a tooth for tooth," [29] and he turned it around. "You have heard it said, 'An eye for an eye and a tooth for a tooth.' but I say to you, if someone strikes you on the right cheek, turn the other also."[30] Jesus' love of the Bible was rich and full! It extended to life-giving texts like Psalm 103:

> *Bless the LORD, O my soul, and do not forget all his bene-fits—*
> *who forgives all your iniquity, who heals all your diseases,*
> *who redeems your life from the pit, who crowns you with*
> *steadfast love and mercy,*
> *who satisfies you with good as long as you live so that your*
> *youth is renewed like the eagle's.*[31]

God doesn't sound at all like a monster here, does God? This is a song of thanksgiving written by one who God has saved from the monsters of this world. Here is the Giver of life, love, and breath. God's blessings here are higher, deeper, broader, and richer than the psalmist ever dreamed possible. This is the real God. This is the God of Jesus. This is the God of love. As people of faith, let's agree not to make God a monster ever again.

Early in 2017, the state of Arkansas announced it would execute eight death row inmates over four days, two executions per day. The state said executions would begin the day

---

29 Deuteronomy 19:21
30 Matthew 5:38-39
31 Psalm 103: 1-5

after Easter Sunday. The state's supply of chemicals for lethal injection was about to expire, and the state did not want to waste it.

During this time, two kinds of Christians spoke up. There were the *God said it, I believe it, that settles it, an eye for an eye and a tooth for a tooth* kind of Christians in favor of moving forward with the executions. And there were the *Bless the Lord, O my soul, and do not forget all God's benefits, who forgives all your iniquity, who heals all your diseases, who redeems your life from the pit* loving kind of Christians.

So, what kind of Christian are you? Is God a monster for you, or is God love?

⁓

Lo, I Am With You Always

This is the day that the Lord has made;
let us rejoice and be glad in it! [32]

TUESDAY, SEPTEMBER 11, 2001, promised to be a perfect day.
I was attending a week-long clergy retreat at Heifer Project
International in Perryville, Arkansas. There was a wonderful
feeling of fall in the air as I rose early in the morning and
jogged the country roads surrounding the retreat center.

Following my run, I returned to my room, showered,
ate breakfast, and headed to the conference center to start
the day's activities. My colleagues and I had just begun our
morning devotionals when a staff member entered the room
and passed a note to one of the participants: *Please pray. A
plane has crashed into the World Trade Center.* With that note,
the earth's axis abruptly tilted, and I knew the world would
never be the same again. My perfect day had come to an end.

God is our refuge and strength,
a very present help in trouble. [33]

---

32   Psalm 118:24
33   Psalm 46:1

The conference ended with news of the terrorist attacks, and I began the three-hour journey home to be with my family. Traveling the interstate, I witnessed automobiles lining the exits as drivers waited to refuel their vehicles at over-crowded gas stations. The terrorist attacks had sparked rumors of limited gasoline supplies.

And when you hear of wars and
rumors of wars, do not be alarmed.[34]

As I continued the journey home, my subconscious mind began cataloging concerns for my country: would there be more attacks on other cities, might so-called "sleeper cells" emerge to frighten the populace further? I thought about fear, the fear many Americans, including myself, were feeling due to these attacks on our native soil. I feared this might be only the first in a series of terrorist actions leveled at the United States.

There is no fear in love, but
perfect love casts out fear.[35]

I thought about hate, the irrational, festering, indescribable hate which resulted in the senseless killing of thousands of innocent people. I also considered the hate many Americans must be feeling for the perpetrators of these horrendous acts.

---

34   Mark 13:7
35   1 John 4:18

Love your enemies and pray
for those who persecute you.[36]

I thought about the loss of innocence for my children, my nation, and myself. Would we ever be able to recapture our childlike faith? Would we ever again be willing to make ourselves vulnerable enough to trust others?

Whoever does not receive the kingdom of God
like a child shall not enter it. [37]

I thought about chaos, the kind of chaos created by terrorism. In my imagination, I envisioned a scene of twisted steel and shattered concrete—carnage where landmarks once stood. I prayed for the countless lives that had been lost. I prayed for the family members and friends left behind to grieve. I asked myself if it might be possible for order to ever emerge from this chaos.

Peace I leave with you;
my peace I give you.[38]

Finally, emotionally and spiritually spent, I arrived at home. Pushing open the front door, I was greeted by an affirming blast of the mundane. I smelled dinner in the oven, heard laundry tumbling in the clothes dryer, and felt the love as I embraced my wife and son. After dinner, we made our way to the church. The journey was now complete. I had come full

---

36   Matt. 5:44
37   Mark 10:15
38   John 14:27

circle—back to that destination I had so desperately needed to reach—back to the assurance that, no matter what happens in my life, I am not alone.

If God is for us, then who can be against us?[39]

On September 11, as we mark the anniversary of the terrorist attacks on our nation, may each of us reach that coveted destination in our hearts—an overwhelming peace assuring us that God is with us always. Thanks be to God!

Lo, I am with you always, to the close of the age.[40]

⌒

---

39 Romans 8:31
40 Matthew 28:20

CHAPTER 4

Far to Go

How Shall We Sing the Lord's Song?

Based on Psalm 137

On Sunday, February 24, 1991, Pulaski Heights United Methodist Church commissioned its first-ever foreign mission team to serve for ten days at a medical clinic in Pignon, Haiti. The following reflection, based on that journey, is dedicated to the people of Haiti and the members of the Pulaski Heights mission team.

This message was later shared at the 1991 annual meeting of the Board of Directors for Heifer Project International. It was also used as a teaching tool at North Carolina State University, Raleigh, NC, in a class, World Population and Food Prospects. The twenty-two-month-old boy mentioned near the end of this message was brought to Arkansas through the cooperation of Pulaski Heights UMC and Arkansas Children's Hospital, where he received life-saving heart surgery.

> *By the waters of Babylon,*
> *there we sat down and wept,*
> *when we remembered Zion ...*
> *How shall we sing the Lord's song in a foreign land?*[41]

---

41   Psalm 137:1-4

Once upon a time, long ago, the nation of Haiti was Zion. Haiti was a nation rich in natural resources. Haiti was a veritable Garden of Eden, a tropical paradise, a promised land, a region blessed by God. Lush forests of mahogany, cedar, papaya, mango, coconut, and cashew covered majestic mountain ranges. Rivers and streams flowed clear and cool. Animals of every shape and size roamed the forests; brilliantly colored birds filled the air. Haiti was Zion.

> *By the waters of Babylon,*
> *there we sat down and wept,*
> *when we remembered Zion ...*
> *How shall we sing the Lord's song in a foreign land?*

Zion is gone. The Garden of Eden has been ravaged; the temple destroyed. That Haiti is no more. Colonization by the Spanish and French, political upheaval, slavery, destruction of the forests, and extreme poverty, all have made Haiti a desolate land today.

Our Pulaski Heights mission team witnessed the ruin firsthand as we flew into Cap-Haitien International Airport in Haiti. From high above in the plane, we saw the mountains laid bare. The mahogany and cedar have been felled to make settees and dining tables for American and European homes.

As soon as we landed on Haitian soil, we were hustled through customs. Our baggage and medical supplies were piled into trucks headed to our destination—the remote village of Pignon and the Hospital de Bienfaisanc—some forty miles south of Cap-Haitien.

As our van sped through the city's streets, our sensibilities were shocked by the sights, sounds, and smells of this the poorest nation in the western hemisphere. Row after row of shanties made of cinder block, tin, and cardboard lined the streets. Street vendors stood on every corner hawking their wares: sugar, candy, stunted vegetables, rancid meat, and stolen bicycle parts. People were everywhere: beggars, the homeless, school children in uniforms, shoppers, wanderers.

Tap-taps (brightly painted Haitian buses) careen down the streets filled beyond capacity, their horns blasting, warning pedestrians to get out of the way. People chase us through the streets shouting, "Blanc, blanc [white man, white man], give me a dollar! Give me a dollar! Don't you want to help me?"

Foul odors meet our nostrils at every turn: raw sewage, human feces, bloated animal carcasses floating in the bay. The city lies in ruin.

> *By the waters of Babylon,*
> *there we sat down and wept,*
> *when we remembered Zion ...*
> *How shall we sing the Lord's song in a foreign land?*

As we left Cap-Haitien and moved into open country, I told myself, "Surely conditions will be better." But the hopelessness that permeates Haiti became even more defined in the desolate landscape of the countryside: treeless vistas, washed-out roads, and shacks were everywhere. Driving along, we came face to face with naked children standing by the roadside eating sugarcane, waiting for nothing. Women walk the dusty road, buckets balanced on their heads, traveling miles on foot to find a sip of water, even contaminated water.

We heard no sound of birds singing in Haiti. The birds and animals had disappeared along with the green forests.

> *By the waters of Babylon,*
> *there we sat down and wept,*
> *when we remembered Zion ...*
> *How shall we sing the Lord's song in a foreign land?*

The people of Haiti must have felt as if they had been abandoned by God. Everywhere we looked, sickness, poverty, and pain flourished in this land. I heard the lament of the psalmist:

> *On the willows there*
> *we hung up our lyres,*
> *for there our captors*
> *required of us songs,*
> *and our tormentors, mirth, saying,*
> *"Sing us one of the songs of Zion!"*[42]

In their exile to Babylon, the Israelites were taunted, teased, and forced by their captor to sing songs through their tears. The people of Haiti also face the music of suffering and torment every day. With a life expectancy of forty-five years, Haitians know the meaning of pain.

We saw the agony everywhere we went. Angelia is only nine years old, but she knows pain. Having suffered from a

---

42   Psalm 137: 2-3

chronic skin disease for most of her life, Angelia was covered with scales and sores. Her skin was badly scarred, the contractures causing her limbs to draw. She walked only with great difficulty. Eyelashes gone, hair matted and thinning, Angelia was an outcast, a leper, in the village of Ranquitte. We loaded her into a pickup truck and delivered her to Pignon to receive medical care.

By the waters of Babylon,
there we sat down and wept,
when we remembered Zion.

The woman lies still and silent in a dirty hospital bed. Early in the day, she delivered a stillborn child—dead two days in her womb. As I look upon her face from behind a veiled curtain, I see her silent suffering—a gauze-wrapped stick clinched between her teeth. In the early morning hours, as I slept, she died. I awoke to the sounds of hammering in the marketplace—the casket maker plying his trade.

By the waters of Babylon,
there we sat down and wept,
when we remembered Zion ...

It was early morning in Pignon. People had begun to gather under the tree that stands between the hospital and the clinic: peddlers, beggars, mothers holding babies with bloated bellies and reddish-tinged hair. The unnatural hair color and ballooning bellies are signs of malnutrition. Most mothers had nothing to feed their children—their own breast milk having dried up. Needy, hungry people gathered at the hospital: people whose need of dental care had been ignored too long. Others afflicted with disease, people sick from drinking contaminated water, those who could not understand their own suffering—they only know they hurt.

With my American definition of what brings happiness and joy—with my personal satisfaction dependent on automobiles, air conditioners, the latest technology in mattresses, the latest movies, and dining out without a thought to the expense, I asked myself: "How can these people possibly go on? How can the people of Haiti ever sing the Lord's song in such a god-forsaken place?"

But as the days passed, as I walked the streets of the village and watched and listened—as I came to know the people—I began to pick up the sound of a faint melody rising from the poverty and squalor of Haiti. The song is soft and low, just barely audible.

I heard the song of children pounding grain into meal in the backyard of a shanty. I heard the music of little boys as they recovered a tin can from a rubbish heap, and they claimed it as a new toy. They beat their "drum" and sang as they marched through the village streets. I heard the song of a wedding party as they paraded to the church, the faces of the bride and groom reflecting hope, promise, and joy. I heard the song of the marketplace: the hustle and bustle of the traders, the braying of donkeys, and the bleating of goats. I listened to the beautiful musical sounds from the Roman Catholic church as children sang praises to God with native songs and bongo drums. I heard the walls of the Baptist Church reverberate with melodic praise as the congregation sang in their native Creole, "Blessed Assurance, Jesus is mine, O what a foretaste of glory divine!"

The song became stronger and stronger. I heard the timbre of a doctor's voice as she comforted a patient in pain. I heard the music of a well being drilled as clean water rushed forth to offer life and hope. I heard the voice of a missionary teaching food preservation methods to women in the countryside, heard the whir of a dentist's drill, and the scraping of rust as hospital beds were prepped for a fresh coat of paint. I heard the pounding of nails as men erected a basketball goal for children.

I heard a song of thanksgiving as a malnourished baby gained an ounce of weight, a song of laughter and tears mingled together as the little girl, Angelia, was bathed and soothed with ointment. A missionary lifted a clean dress over her shoulders as volunteers decorated the girl's hair with multicolored ribbons. I remember being present as a clean dress was placed on her body, and ribbons were tied in her hair by a missionary. Angelia received the gift of a mirror that reflected her beauty. She saw herself as something entirely new—someone who can be beautiful. She smiled.

In memory, the songs go on and on and on until they seem to swell into a celebratory symphony of hope, love, and grace.

The people of Haiti sing the Lord's song every day. But if the song is to continue, there is much to be done. Reforestation programs are needed—agricultural help is a must. There is a desperate need for more water wells and health clinics. Teachers and educators are in demand everywhere. The people of Haiti are hungry for partners who will share the love of Jesus Christ with committed hands and hearts.

How shall we sing the Lord's song in a foreign land?

His father carried him into the clinic. The little boy, only twenty-two months old, was tired and listless. Our doctors determined the boy was suffering from heart disease. Without surgery, his father was told, the child may not live to sing a song on his third birthday. We understood that someone must transport him to the United States to provide medical care. Otherwise, the casket maker may, once again, be busy in the marketplace.

From the time Haiti touched me, it was clear that I could never forget the people of the island nation. The images remain with me, years after my departure.

If I forget you, O Jerusalem,
Let my right hand wither!
Let my tongue cleave to the roof
Of my mouth, if I do not remember you.[43]

When the time came to leave Pignon, we loaded our baggage on the tap-tap. One of the local boys, a beggar, approached me and asked a question:

"Pastor, do you love Haiti?"

"Yes, I love Haiti very much."

"Will you come back to us?"

"I hope to come back someday."

"Remember me."

If I forget you, O Jerusalem, O Haiti,
let my right hand wither.
Let my tongue cleave to the roof
of my mouth, if I do not remember you."

How shall we sing the Lord's song in a foreign land?

---

43   Psalm 137:5-6

Hunger

Based on Matthew 14: 13-21

We met on Red Square in Moscow. I was strolling along the Kremlin wall near Lenin's tomb late one afternoon when I spied him. He began to follow closely on my heels, his eyes darting to make sure no one was watching. I slowed my pace to allow him to catch up with me. Finally, standing face-to-face with one another, he whispered in broken English, "Are you American?"

"Yes," I responded, "What do you want?"

"You want to buy nice Russian souvenir to take home to the USA?" he asked.

"Sure," I replied. With that, he began pulling samples of hand-painted Russian trinkets from his coat pockets. I was in the company of a Russian black-market trader!

I searched and found a souvenir I admired, so I asked my Soviet friend how much it would cost me. He responded, "One Michael Jordan t-shirt, please." When I informed him that not all Americans own a Michael Jordan t-shirt, his eyes were drawn to the sunglasses perched atop my head. He pointed to them and asked, "What about those?" No sooner had I indicated my willingness to trade for my sunglasses than my black-market trader hailed a cab, shoved me into the back seat, jumped in beside me, and we sped away through the streets of the city.

He began speaking to the driver in Russian, even as I shouted at them, "Speak English! Speak English! I don't understand! Where are you taking me? Where are we going?" I pleaded for an answer.

"My apartment. We are going to my apartment for souvenirs," he responded. And so I settled back in the car seat and tried to relax as we drove for what seemed like an eternity.

It was well past my dinner time. It was getting late, and I suddenly became aware of a rumbling in the pit of my stomach. The car halted in front of a dilapidated tenement building at the edge of the city. My new friend pulled me from the back seat and hustled me through a weedy lot toward his apartment building. Once inside he warned, "Don't speak until we are in my home."

"Why?" I asked.

"Because I was taken into custody last week for having another American in my apartment," he replied. Suddenly, I imagined myself sitting in a Soviet prison, and my mug shot plastered on the front page of *Pravda*.

As we entered the elevator, an old babushka, a Russian peasant woman, stared at me with suspicious eyes. Getting off on the seventh floor, we passed through three locked doors, finally reaching the hovel my friend called home. I was a basket case. Here I was alone in a foreign country—the Soviet

Union no less—with, for all I knew, a convicted Russian felon. No one knew my whereabouts. I didn't even know my whereabouts! I was filled with fear and a pang of terrible, aching hunger.

But then my friend spoke, "Are you hungry? Let me fix you something to eat." He reached into the cupboard, pulled out an old coffee pot and a couple of chipped mugs, and with his last bit of coffee from the bottom of a rusty canister, fixed us a hot drink. That evening as we sat around the table sharing our lives, our cultures, our families, and our experiences, my anxiety faded, and my hunger was satisfied.

ᴄ

It was another late afternoon long ago beside the sea of Galilee. A crowd had gathered to hear Jesus teach. All day long, they had come, more than five thousand people, men, women, and children. Jesus amazed the crowd with his wisdom and his miracles of healing. Everyone wanted to touch him, look into his eyes and hear his voice. But now it was late, and the people wanted something else. Now they were hungry. Their stomachs were empty, and they craved food.

The disciples begged Jesus to send the crowd away. "We have nothing to offer them. We've only managed to scrape together five loaves and two fish."

But Jesus said, "No, we will feed them." Taking the five loaves and two fish, he looked up to heaven, blessed and broke the bread, and gave it to the disciples to set before the crowd. All five thousand ate that day, and their stomachs were filled.

Have you ever been hungry? Truly hungry? Few of us know firsthand the terrible experience of intense hunger. Few of us know bread lines and soup kitchens. Few of us have held out an empty tin cup to receive a sip of water. Few of us can relate to the grim photos we see in the media of third-world children with their sunken eyes and hollow cheeks, marionette arms, and calf-less legs. This kind of hunger is beyond our comprehension.

In my own family, the dinner conversation doesn't center so much around how hungry we are. Rather, it centers around calorie intake. What's it going to be tonight? What is the diet of the week? Believe me. I've accumulated an impressive list during the course of my life: Nutra-system, Scarsdale diet, grapefruit diet, carrot sticks and celery… Who hasn't tried at least one quicky weight loss gimmick? Of course, for every bowl of ice cream I eat, I must do penance by running five miles to burn away the excess calories.

My five-year-old son wanders into the bathroom to watch me shave in the morning. As I stand before the mirror, naked from the waist up, he innocently remarks, "Gee, Dad, you're getting fat," and I'm thrown into a tailspin. "What do you mean I'm getting fat! I'm not fat at all! Look at me! There's not an ounce of fat on my body!" But the seed of doubt has been planted, so I skip breakfast, lunch, and dinner in an attempt to remedy the problem. By 7 p.m., there's a gnawing, nagging emptiness in my stomach. By 8 p.m., my head begins to ache, and I feel dizzy. By 9 p.m., I fear that I'm going to die.

The hunger pangs are intense. By 10 p.m., I'm ready to go to an all-night diner for the Blue Plate Special—anything to cure the terrible hunger I feel in my gut.

Because we are all members of the human family, we are also familiar with another kind of hunger that has nothing to do with our position on the ideal weight chart. We can be overweight or underweight, obese or emaciated, pleasingly plump, or model slim. We can be health food freaks or junk food addicts, but this particular kind of hunger afflicts all of us. It is with us when we get up in the morning and when we go to bed at night. It is with us before we eat and even after we push ourselves away from the table. This particular hunger is a hunger for God.

The gospels remind us that we need the "gift of bread" to sustain life. But even more than bread, the scriptures tell us we need the "gift of God" to give our lives meaning, purpose, and direction. After Jesus fed the multitude near the sea of Galilee, they followed him. They followed him all the way to Capernaum. In Capernaum, on the steps of the synagogue, the throng asked Jesus for a second helping of fish and loaves to satisfy their hunger. But Jesus reminded the people that what they needed most was not a second helping of food, but rather a balanced diet. "Very truly, I say to you, you are only here for another free meal. Don't chase after the food that perishes. Look instead for the food that endures to eternal life; the food that is truly filling."

Psychologists have argued that the hunger we feel in our

stomachs is closely tied to the longing we feel in our hearts. Often our efforts to either build ourselves up or slim ourselves down are nothing more than a search for that elusive thing we call fulfillment.

I've come to realize that my personal eating habits are a reflection of my emotional and spiritual health. My weight serves as a kind of barometer for how I am doing in my life. If things are going smoothly and I am in tune with God, I eat sensibly, and I exercise. However, during those periods when I am out of touch with God and neighbors, my cholesterol count shoots sky-high from consuming too much junk food, and I find myself loosening my belt an additional notch.

The good news, however, is that Jesus Christ offers to fill our deepest hunger—the insatiable hunger within our souls. Christ has the power to take away our hurt, pain, stress, and disappointment and instead fill our emptiness with love, joy, peace, and hope. Jesus said, "I am the bread of life. Whoever comes to me will never be hungry. And whoever believes in me will never be thirsty."

⁓

It was late afternoon in another place and time when I found myself walking down a dusty road in Haiti. Suddenly, I was surrounded by a crowd of children. They followed along, tugging and pulling at me, fascinated by this foreigner in their midst. I couldn't help but notice their stick-like arms and legs, their bloated bellies and sick eyes, all signs of malnutrition. "Are you hungry? Would you like something to eat?" I asked, pulling a package of cheese crackers from my backpack. I handed it to a little girl and watched as she carefully tore open the cellophane wrapper and began to divide the crackers. First, she broke them in half, then into quarters, and finally into even smaller pieces until she finally had enough morsels to share with everyone present. That day, on that dusty road, everybody's hunger was satisfied.

This is my body broken for you. This is my blood shed for you.[44]

Jesus Christ satisfies the hungry heart: in Moscow, in Haiti, and here.

⁓

---

44   1 Corinthians 11

"Without Borders"

BASED ON JOHN 17: 17-26

A journey of a thousand miles begins with one step.[45]

THE OLD PROVERB HAS THE RING OF TRUTH TO IT, doesn't it? More often than not, the first step in any endeavor is the most daunting. In my own personal journeys, both real and imagined, the step I always fear most is the first step. Moving from a familiar place to a new and unknown location leaves me feeling uncertain and insecure.

Suitcase and passport in hand, I trembled as I approached the border station. The uniformed officer demanded my papers, and I presented them. Would I be allowed to cross or not? Even now, after years of border crossings, including a harrowing adventure at the infamous Checkpoint Charlie that divided East and West Berlin during the Cold War, I still sweat whenever I cross an international boundary line.

It happened again as I crossed from the USA into Canada on a wilderness fishing trip. My buddies and I pulled up to the checkpoint where the uniformed attendant took our passports

---

45   This proverb is generally attributed to 6th-century Chinese philosopher Lao Tzu.

and drivers' licenses. The official looked at our documents, stared us up and down, and then asked us to pull over and come inside while they ran a background check.

Oh no! I told myself. Canada is tough on crime! They won't allow anyone with a DUI, a felony conviction, or, in many cases, even a misdemeanor to enter the country. I wracked my brain. Do I have any of these on my record? I couldn't recall any, but the angst was still present. Fortunately, everything checked out, and we were soon on our way to the wilds of Ontario.

These incidents and others remind me of the anxiety that God's people have felt over the years as they crossed border after border in search of a better life. Consider the Israelites' first steps as they followed Joshua into the Promised Land. Or how about the disciples' halting steps as they dropped every-thing to follow Jesus? And then more recently, there are the 57,000 children from El Salvador, Honduras, and Guatemala who crossed the US border by themselves, leaving behind neglect, abuse, and possible death in search of life and love.

What we have before us in the seventeenth chapter of John's gospel is the single most crucial piece of border crossing information in the history of humanity:

> *I ask not only on behalf of these, but also on behalf of those who will believe in me through their word, that they may all be one. As you, Father, are in me and I am in you, may they also be in us, so that the world may believe that you have sent me. The glory that you have given me, I have given them, so*

that they may be one, as we are one, I in them and you in
me, that they may become completely one, so that the world
may know that you have sent me and have loved them even
as you have loved me.[46]

Known as the high priestly prayer of Jesus, these verses
come at the end of Jesus' farewell message to his disciples. The
setting is that last fateful Thursday evening before Jesus' arrest.
He has told the twelve that he will leave them very soon. He
will cross the ultimate border. He will be arrested. He will
be crucified. He will die. First, Jesus shares a meal with his
friends, their last meal together. Next, he washes their feet,
giving them a new commandment, to love one another as he
has loved them. Finally, he prays this prayer before going out
to meet his destiny.

Jesus prays for himself first, and then he prays for his
disciples. Finally, in these verses before us, he does something
remarkable. Jesus prays for us. He prays for you. He prays for
me. He prays for all who will believe in and follow him, and
he even prays for those who will never believe. And what does
he pray? Jesus prays that we might be one, that we might live
our lives without the borders that separate us.

Jesus rejected the categories that separated the people of
his day: Jews from Gentiles, scribes from tax collectors, Pharisees from prostitutes, priests from lepers. Jesus also rejects
the divisions that separate us still today: male from female,

rich from poor, educated from uneducated, gay from straight, liberal from conservative, Tea Party Republicans from Obama/Pelosi Democrats, saints from sinners, orthodox from heretics.

I could go on and on with a list of the borders that separate us, but by and large, they are borders of our own making. Whether we're willing to admit it or not, the boundaries we establish are almost always created to favor ourselves—to put ourselves in a good light—to reassure ourselves that we're OK and those other people are not. And God forgives us. We Christians can be some of the worst border Nazis!

Recently, I read a Facebook post in which a devout, right-thinking follower of Jesus railed against another follower of Jesus for a stance he had taken on a certain hot-potato political issue: "You are the most idiotic, stupid, misguided person I've ever known!" the devout believer wrote, "I can't believe you call yourself a Christian. You're an abomination to the Lord! I pray you'll see the light and find Jesus. God bless you, and have a good day."

It looks like we Christians still have a long way to go, huh?

The good news is that it's not all up to us. Please take note: this prayer is not a conversation between Jesus and you or Jesus and me. Jesus is not telling us that we need to do this or do that. Instead, it's a conversation between Jesus and his heavenly Father. The unity that Jesus desires here is not something you and I can create. It comes from God through the work of the Holy Spirit. It's a unity that transcends mere tolerance. It's about so much more than just getting along or simply being polite to one another. It's about having a deep and abiding love and respect for every single human being on this planet because Jesus died for all, and Jesus loves us all the same. It's a love without borders.

After my buddies and I crossed the Canadian border and eventually arrived at our wilderness campsite located sixty miles from nowhere, we discovered we would be sharing the camp with another species. No, I'm not talking about caribou or elk. I'm talking about another kind of human species. While the four of us were men of a certain age and distinction, the other group consisted of six young, tattooed skateboarders in an adjacent cabin.

"Oh, this'll be an interesting week!" I told myself. "Everything will work out just fine as long as they stay on their side of the border and we stay on ours. And yet, as the week unfolded, we began to cross the line. A member of our group taught the members of the skater group how to clean fish more efficiently. When our drinking water supply ran low, they shared their water with us. When they caught no fish, we presented them with a platter of delicious fried walleye for dinner. In a wonderful sort of way, we became one, and by the end of the week, we all agreed that we'd get together again during the same week next year. I can't wait!

Jesus prayed that we might all be one.

A journey of a thousand miles begins with one step.

Take that first step and keep it simple.

LOVE EVERYBODY.

∽

CHAPTER 5

Loving and Giving

Margie the Priest

BASED ON 1 PETER 2: 4-10

THE GENESIS OF THIS MESSAGE began with a memorial service I preached for a beloved church member, Marjorie Merle Haynes, at Henderson United Methodist Church in Little Rock on September 22, 1994. Later, this homily would morph into a full-fledged sermon preached at First United Methodist Church of Springdale on January 12, 2003. Still later, I would take this same message and create a new piece for the dedication of the newly constructed gathering hall, sky bridge, and renovated children and youth areas at Pulaski Heights UMC in Little Rock on September 11, 2015.

We met in the receiving line following worship. I was the new preacher, and she was a member of my new flock. She told me she liked my sermon; she said I reminded her of a Presbyterian pastor she once knew in Colorado. To be honest, she reminded me of no one I'd ever known in my life. While she may not have fallen under the category of savant syndrome, you know, people who are seriously deficient in some cognitive areas while being startlingly brilliant in others—still Margie was my "rain man."

Margie's brain was wired differently, perhaps uniquely.

Her reality was not the reality of your average Joe. Margie marched to the beat of a different drum. Like most people, she could see "point A" and "point B," but unlike most of us who typically take the direct route from one point to another, Margie's mental routes were more circuitous.

As a child, Margie struggled through school. She never graduated high school. Margie received a certificate of attendance instead. In the days before political correctness, Margie was thought to be slow, stupid, and even retarded. Life did not come easy for Margie. And yet, what she may have lacked in grey matter, she more than made up for in determination and guts. It took years, but Margie eventually earned her GED, repeating some portions of the test as many as four times before she finally passed.

Later, Margie joined Toastmasters International to fine-tune her public speaking skills. She also became a consumer advocate, once spending months corresponding with a potato chip company after she bought a bag of stale chips. Her efforts eventually paid off, and she received more free potato chips than she could handle.

At one point in her life, out of work and money, Margie began painting original works of art on canvas with mascara and nail polish. She put them up for sale and marketed them as "Cosmetic Art by Margie." Margie even went through literacy training, and ultimately the one who struggled to read herself ended up teaching others how to read.

Margie was amazingly gifted. She had the rare ability to

remember everything, and I do mean everything, from dates and places to times and minute details from the past. Margie could quote lengthy passages from my sermons verbatim. She never forgot anything! "Britt," Margie would say in her Margie voice, "when are you going to loan me that book about grace you promised?" "I never promised any such thing, Margie!" I responded. "Yes, you did, eight months ago on October fourteenth at 1:20 p.m. We were standing in the hallway outside your office. I was wearing my blue dress, and you were trying to avoid me!"

Margie could be difficult at times, but she gave so much of herself. When she joined the church, she promised the congregation to be present every Sunday unless she was sick or away on vacation. Margie kept that promise. Margie served meals to the homeless in the inner city. She was active in her Sunday school class, and she attended every church potluck. She played in the handbell choir though she couldn't read a lick of music, and she had no discernable sense of rhythm. Margie was a giver. She didn't expect much in return—she just gave.

For me, knowing Margie left me with conflicted feelings. On the one hand, I told myself, "Thank God I'm not like Margie," while on the other hand, I admitted to myself, "I wish to God I could be more like Margie."

And then one night, while Margie was watching TV, her heart stopped beating. Our faith community felt the loss keenly. We were left feeling a gaping hole that Margie had once filled so perfectly. In a sense, Margie had been Christ in our midst—the one who came, led a simple life of service, and gave until there was nothing left to give. Margie even gave beyond her death. Her organ donor card read, "I give my body or my organs (or both if needed)." At her memorial service, only her handbell rested on the altar. Margie ministered to us and challenged us. She made us more human—more compassionate—more holy. Margie had been our "priest" in the truest sense of the word.

> *Come to him, a living stone, though rejected by mortals yet chosen and precious in God's sight, and like living stones, let yourselves be built into a spiritual house, to be a holy priesthood, to offer spiritual sacrifices acceptable to God through Jesus Christ.*[47]

Written near the end of the first century AD, the letter we know as First Peter was composed during a time of great upheaval in the church. The Jerusalem temple had been destroyed, stone by stone, and animal sacrifices had ceased. Christians were martyred, and the church was reeling— needing something to hold on to in uncertain times. This is precisely what the author of First Peter provides. He reminds his readers, both then and now, that the church is not a geographical location. It is not a temple, brand-new gathering hall, or even a recently constructed sky bridge. The faith is not built of bricks and mortar. Instead, it consists of living stones:

---

47   1 Peter 2: 4-5

Jesus Christ is our temple and chief cornerstone, and we also are living stones gathered around him to be the church alive.

> *But you are a chosen race, a royal priesthood, a holy nation, God's own people, in order that you may proclaim the mighty acts of him who called you out of darkness into his marvelous light. Once you were not a people, but now you are God's people; once you had not received mercy, but now you have received mercy.*[48]

In other words, when we are baptized, we move from darkness to light. We move from being nobodies to somebodies. We are given the power to transform the world. We are ordained. We become priests! This ordination is true not only for those of us who wear clergy vestments, but for all of us. We are all priests called to lead, teach, care for, and share the faith.

Several weeks after Margie died, I received a phone call from her sister, Fran. Fran didn't go to church. She didn't believe. She was somewhat skeptical. "For years," Fran told me, "I listened as Margie talked about the church. She told me she was praying for me, but I resisted. Now Margie is gone, and I feel empty. The church was wonderful to Margie, both in life and in death. The love was incredible. I'm ready to believe now. I'm ready to be baptized. I'm ready to be part of the church."

So, Fran was baptized and joined the church along with her husband, Bruce. Together, they taught, gave, and served most remarkably. In essence, Margie did not leave us empty.

---

48   1 Peter 2: 9-10

She sent her sister Fran to be a priest.

We need more priests! We need more Margies! We need you because transforming the world for Jesus Christ is an arduous task. It requires a group effort. Thank you for your love. Thank you for your giving. Thank you for your service. Thank you for your witness. Together we are changing the world, one person at a time.

You Made My Day!

BASED ON JOHN 4: 4-15

Go ahead! Make my day!

IT'S ONE OF THE MOST RECOGNIZABLE catchphrases on the planet. First uttered by none other than Dirty Harry Callahan, aka Clint Eastwood, in the 1983 action film *Sudden Impact,* we all know what it means, don't we? It means precisely what it says: "Go ahead! Make my day! Just do it! Step across this line! Knock this chip off my shoulder! I double-dog dare you!" It's a statement of aggression that I recommend you not use anytime, anywhere, with anyone.

There is, however, an almost identical-sounding catchphrase that I would encourage you to use all the time with everyone possible. Rather than *make my day,* try using *you made my day* instead. "You made my day" acknowledges that someone has lifted your spirits and made your day brighter and better.

Whenever a child approaches me at the conclusion of Sunday morning worship and presents me with a crayon drawing or a handmade pipe cleaner trinket, I automatically hug that youngster and exclaim, "Thank you! You made my day!"

Just this past week, I was visiting an out-of-town viewer of our televised worship broadcast in the hospital when he said to me, "You look much younger in person than you do on TV."

Of course, I responded, "Aww, you made my day!"

And here's the thing about using this particular catch-phrase. When we tell someone they made our day, it makes our day as well. When we lift up others, we feel lifted up ourselves. When we fill the buckets of others to the brim, we end up having our bucket filled in the process. The "water supply" is unlimited!

I fear that today we live in a culture in which filling the buckets of others is rapidly giving way to name-calling and denigration. I was fortunate. I grew up in an era of hope and optimism. Everyone liked Ike, and everyone from my parents to my grandparents to the neighbors seemed happy to fill the buckets of my young self. Even TV personalities like Captain Kangaroo, Andy Griffith, and Walter Cronkite left me feeling confident.

I can recall a period in my childhood when my bucket felt chronically depleted. It was my first-grade year, and I was a shy kid with perfectionist tendencies. More than anything, I wanted to please my teacher. Unfortunately, she was impossible to please. One day I made an error in my "Dick and Jane" reading workbook. Feeling terrible, I carried it up to my teacher's desk, hoping to receive some much-needed reassurance that my failure had not been fatal. However, when she saw it, my teacher took on the frightening persona of an old crone and, in a voice loud enough for all my classmates to hear, screamed, "You ruined it! You've marred your workbook forever! Don't ever forget your mistake!" Believe me, I haven't. Sixty years later, I still hold on to that Dick and Jane reading workbook with the terrible mistake inside.

Study after study shows that if we want our children to thrive, we must *make their day* with reinforcing affirmations. We must stop beating up on our children for their mistakes. Instead of criticizing them for the "C" they made in math, praise them instead for the "A" they made in English. We must help them identify their strengths to make sure their buckets will be filled in the future. We must do the same in all our relationships, as well. Perhaps the greatest example of this is found in Jesus' encounter with the woman at the well.

> *So Jesus came to a Samaritan city called Sychar, near the plot of ground that Jacob had given to his son Joseph. Jacob's well was there, and Jesus, tired out by his journey, was sitting by the well. It was about noon. A Samaritan woman came to draw water, and Jesus said to her, "Give me a drink."*
> *The Samaritan woman said to him, "How is it that you, a Jew, ask a drink of me, a woman of Samaria?"*
> *Jesus answered her, "If you knew the gift of God, and who it is that is saying to you, 'Give me a drink,' you would have asked him, and he would have given you living water."*[49]

---

49   John 4: 5-10

In a time and place where bucket filling was rare—in a culture where lepers were required to cry "unclean" as they moved from place to place—where women were admonished to hide behind screens in the synagogue, segregated and hidden from men—in a world where the only good Samaritan was a dead Samaritan, at least as far as the Hebrews were concerned, Jesus broke down barriers that separated people. Jesus ignored long-held social and religious restrictions that had kept people apart for centuries. Wherever he went, Jesus proclaimed the good news that "God is love and God loves every human being just the same."

At a place called Sychar, Jesus encounters a Samaritan woman at Jacob's well. Both Jesus and the woman show incredible courage in this meeting. One brave and thirsty man dares to ask for a drink of water from one whose gender, race, and religion make her the wrong person to give it to him. One brave and generous woman dares to provide a drink of water to one whose gender, race, and religion make him the wrong one to receive it.

Whether accidental or intentional, Awkward encounters have the power to make our day and change us forever. It certainly changed the life of the Samaritan woman. Jesus so filled her spiritual bucket that she arose, left her physical bucket behind, and went forth to brighten the days of others.

When someone invites us to step up and do something beyond our comfort zone, they aren't emptying our bucket. Instead, they're "making our day" by forcing us to draw deeply within ourselves. What does it mean to be faithful? What does it mean to defend the orphan? What does it mean to embrace the immigrant? What does it mean to fight for healthcare for those who have none? What does it mean to care for and build up those whose buckets are empty? How will we make their day? These are the questions we must continually ask ourselves.

When I began my freshman year of college in the fall of 1972, it didn't take long before I realized I was still that same first-grade boy terrified of making a mistake in his Dick and Jane workbook. Oh, I looked the part of Joe College with my platform shoes, pleated pants, polyester shirt, and sports car. On the inside, however, my bucket was empty.

One day in the cafeteria line, I spotted her in front of me—a seeing impaired co-ed. Not only was she blind, but her demeanor was not very cool at all, at least by my flawed standards. She was fumbling around with her food tray and her white cane. Before I knew it, she raised her voice and asked, "Could you help me, please?"

I wanted to ignore her. I tried to pretend I'd never heard her. After all, she couldn't see me, and I didn't want to look like a geek in front of my fellow freshmen. Still, I helped her. I picked up her food tray as she took my arm, and together we found a table. I had filled her bucket, and she had filled mine in a way I never dreamed possible.

She made my day! She made my day!

⌒

Let Go of Fear

Based on 1 John 4: 7-21

Perfect love casts out fear.

FROM THE MOMENT OF OUR BIRTH, we are drawn to other human beings like a moth to a flame. We have been divinely created to connect with others, to love and be loved. As we are rocked, fed, and lullabied to sleep as infants, we naturally grow in this love until we eventually repeat the same cycle of rocking, feeding, and lullabying others ourselves. Love is the most powerful of all human emotions. I cannot recall a time when I did not feel loved. Love has always been with me.

But what about fear? How does fear enter our lives? Fear is different from love, isn't it? Fear typically rears its ugly head later in our development, most often when we find ourselves threatened and backed into a corner. While love makes us feel alive, fear makes us feel vulnerable, fragile, and finite.

My first-ever memory of fear is vivid. I can still recall when and where I was when I felt this unsettling emotion. It happened fifty years ago inside a guest room at the Sands Motel in Meridian, Mississippi. It was the summer of 1964, a pivotal time in the American civil rights movement often referred to as *Freedom Summer*. More than seven hundred civil rights workers from across the nation had traveled to Mississippi to combat discrimination at the polls by registering African American voters.

On June 21, three young civil rights workers, James Chaney, Andrew Goodman, and Mickey Schwerner, drove from Meridian to the town of Philadelphia, Mississippi, to investigate the burning of the Mt. Zion Methodist Church. They never returned to Meridian. These three young martyrs vanished, along with the car they were driving. The eyes of the nation were focused on Mississippi as stories of racism, hate, lynching, and murder emerged. The Civil Rights Act was signed two weeks after the disappearance of Chaney, Goodman, and Schwerner, and their bodies were found three weeks after the signing on August 4, 1964.

In the midst of this turmoil, my mother, grandmother, three brothers, and I found ourselves traveling the two-lane roads of rural Mississippi on our way to vacation along the Florida gulf coast. Ominous radio broadcasts and hushed conversations between my mom and my grandmother in the front seat of the car let me know they were feeling apprehensive. No sooner had we checked into the Sands Motel that evening than my mom rushed to close the curtains and double-lock the door. My brothers and I were warned not to open that door under any circumstances.

It may sound strange today, but it was the first time in my life I remembered sleeping behind a locked door. I was ten years old. We never locked our doors at home. We never even considered it. On this particular night, however, the door was locked. Fear had entered my life in a palpable way.

Beloved, let us love one another because love is from God; everyone who loves is born of God and knows God. Whoever does not love does not know God, for God is love. God's love was revealed among us in this way: God sent his only son into the world so that we might live through him. In this is love, not that we loved God but that he loved us and sent his Son to be the atoning sacrifice for our sins. Beloved, since God loved us so much, we also ought to love one another.[50]

Has there ever been a letter so heavily saturated with the language of love? The recipients of this epistle must surely have felt they were being rocked, fed, and lullabied to sleep. The author repeatedly refers to his readers as beloved. The word "love" is used no less than twenty-six times over the course of only fourteen verses. This passage echoes the classic words of John 3:16: "For God so loved the world that he gave his only son, that whoever believes in him may not perish but have eternal life." Through the gift of Jesus Christ, we need not fear. God is with us! God loves us! And because God loves us, we can love one another. It's as simple as that!

Unfortunately, not all of the recipients of John's letter were feeling the love. There were divisions and fear among the body of believers to whom this letter was written. Some had left the church. Some were feeling shaky in their faith. We

---

50   1 John 4:7-11

don't know why. Some scholars believe there may have been a disagreement over the nature of Christ's divinity versus his humanity. While everyone embraced the divinity of Jesus—his love—his deep and abiding connection with God, some could not embrace the human side of Jesus—the Jesus who felt emotions like doubt, anxiety, and fear.

Whatever the reason for the divisions, John issued an impassioned plea for love, "How can we love [a] God we haven't seen," John writes, "if we can't love our sisters and brothers [whom] we have seen?" "Let go of your fear!" John tells the church, "Let go! Unlock the doors! Tear down the walls! Throw out the welcome mat! Embrace one another!"

"God is love." This is the simple message of First John. Please note: John doesn't say "Love is God." After all, many kinds of love are not of God. No, John is talking here about a crucified love—a love that is willing to step out and take risks by feeding the hungry, clothing the naked, emptying the bed pans, and, yes, even registering disenfranchised voters.

St. Francis of Assisi is often attributed for writing these wise words:

> For it is in giving that we receive, it is in pardoning that we are
> pardoned, and it is in loving that we are loved.[51]

In her memoir, Carolyn Goodman, mother of Andrew

---

51   Contemporary scholars have established that the famous "Peace Prayer," although it embodies the spirit of St. Francis of Assisi, is not one of his writings. The prayer first appeared during World War I, written on the back of a holy card with a picture of St. Francis on it. Retrieved from https://franciscan-archive.org/patriarcha/peace.html

Goodman, the youngest of the three civil rights workers murdered at the age of twenty, admitted that she was afraid for her son to leave their home in New York City to go to Mississippi in the summer of '64. "But he wanted to be a beacon of light in the heart of darkness," Goodman wrote of her child, "how could I deny him?" Perfect love casts out fear.

It's still with us today, isn't it—the hate and fear? Hate and fear between Russia and Ukraine, hate and fear between Israel and Palestine, or hate and fear along the US / Mexican border. We need God's perfect love to cast out the fear, don't we? But where do we begin? Where do we start? It's all so overwhelming. How about starting right here? How about just trying to love the person whose driving irritates you, the loudmouth who supports an opposing political candidate, or the parent whose child interrupts your Sunday morning meditation?

⌒

CHAPTER 6

Works Hard for a Living

Flying and Falling

BASED ON GENESIS 9: 18-29

DREAMS ARE THOSE IMAGES, IDEAS, AND EMOTIONS that occur during what is scientifically known as the REM—rapid eye movement—stage of sleep. All of us dream, though we remember very few of our dreams. Most of us accept the Freudian idea that dreams offer insight into our hidden desires and emotions. In other words, different dreams mean different things depending on our state of mind. For example, the dream of flying—soaring high above the earth—touching the stars—swooping and diving—symbolizes liberation from our worries by rising above the fray. The dream of flying is joy-filled.

The dream of falling, on the other hand, can be disturbing. Falling in real life is not something we choose to do, and yet it happens from time to time. When we fall, we feel embarrassed. We look around to see if anyone is watching. Dreams of falling symbolize anxiety and helplessness, of being pushed beyond our comfort zone.

And then there are those dreams that involve both flying and falling. In these dreams, we soar high above the clouds on eagles' wings, but then we plummet to earth and crash. Dreams of flying and falling symbolize our fear of losing everything we've worked so hard to gain, a loss of control.

When I think of flying and falling, I think of addiction. Addiction, by definition, is a condition that occurs when someone abuses a substance like alcohol or drugs or engages excessively in an activity like gambling or sex. What seems pleasurable and harmless at first soon becomes chronic and compulsive. At some point, it interferes with the normal flow of life, including our relationships, careers, and even our physical health. If not treated, the addicted quickly move from flying high to falling and bottoming out.

We can become addicted to almost anything: alcohol, tobacco, drugs, gambling, pornography, food, retail therapy, even our cell phones! I hail from a long line of addictive personalities, those who are inclined to get hooked at the drop of a pin. My sainted grandmother, God rest her soul, had her addictions. No, she wasn't addicted to alcohol or drugs. My grandmother's cravings were more socially acceptable. She had an unnatural obsession with Vicks VapoRub®. She slathered it on anything and everything, including me, when I was a child. There was also her addiction to candy orange slices. She couldn't get enough of them. Later in life, she became hooked on wheat germ. She was convinced it was the fountain of youth, and if she just ate enough, she would live forever.

Personally, I can't be in the same room with dark chocolate. If I get my hands on it, I devour it. Yes, I know. Dark chocolate possesses certain health benefits for human beings, but not at the toxic levels I would consume—if all barriers were dropped!

Physicians and psychologists don't completely agree on the source of our addictions. Is it physical? Is it the release of dopamine in the brain? Perhaps it's emotional? Or maybe it's some hidden personality trait? No one knows for sure. However, there is one thing we do know. We know that those who struggle with addiction, and in this nation, that's approximately forty million people, don't do it simply to experience a cheap thrill. Addiction has nothing to do with morality or strength of character.

As a pastor, I have found that those who struggle with addiction are often among the brightest, most sensitive, and most moral people I know. They just seem to have this proclivity for addiction in the same way I have my father's receding hairline, or some have their mother's Roman nose.

Unfortunately, the church hasn't always viewed it this way. While we love to quote St. Augustine, who said, "the church is not a hotel for saints, but a hospital for sinners," we often convey the opposite message. We put up such a respectful façade that it frightens away those who are even mildly flawed. They feel they must be perfect before the church will embrace them.

In his letter to the Romans (3:23) Paul wrote, "For all have sinned and fall short of the glory of God." The truth is, we're all broken, every last one of us. I'm broken. You're broken. Some of us just hide it better than others.

What we have before us in this odd little story from Genesis is proof that we're all in the same broken boat. We all stand in need of the same kind of redemption that comes from God and God alone.

> *The sons of Noah who went out of the ark were Shem, Ham, and Japheth. These three were the sons of Noah, and from these, the whole earth was peopled. Noah, a man of the soil, was the first to plant a vineyard. He drank some of the wine and became drunk, and he lay uncovered in his tent. And Ham, the father of Canaan, saw the nakedness of his father, and told his two brothers outside.*[52]

Noah's resume in the early chapters of Genesis reads like that of a saint—he was upright, blameless, the best of the best, the crème de la crème. Sadly, however, the world had become so evil and broken that God decided to send a flood to destroy every living creature on the planet—save for Noah, his family, and a cluster of living creatures housed on a floating ark. God chose this remnant to represent a new beginning for the world.

After the rains ended and the floodwaters began to subside, a dove was sent out from the ark. The dove didn't return. The boat eventually landed on solid ground. Noah, his family, and all the living creatures aboard then disembarked. A rainbow appeared in the sky, and everyone lived happily forever after. Well, not quite. What I love and admire most about God is this: God could've ended the story here. God could've kept it all nice and pretty, but God didn't. Instead,

---

52 Genesis 9:18, 19-22

God chose to speak the truth, the whole truth, and nothing but the truth.

As the late Paul Harvey would say, "Here's the rest of the story,[53]" compliments of God. After Noah left the boat, he planted a vineyard, harvested the grapes, made a batch of wine, became drunk, found himself naked and passed out in his tent. Noah crashed and burned. So, this is God's crème de la creme? Of course, this didn't happen overnight. Years passed while Noah planted that vineyard, tended the vines as they matured, waited years for it to bear fruit, years before he could harvest the grapes, years for the grapes to ferment and become wine, and years to feed his addiction.

But patience is not the most important lesson of this story. What is most important here is not what Noah did, but rather what his sons did—how they responded to their father's addiction. While Ham ridicules his dad by gawking at his embarrassing situation and laughing at him, Shem and Japheth choose to guard their father's dignity. They cover his nakedness. They care for him and nurture him back to wholeness. They help Noah learn to fly again.

Shem and Japheth demonstrated our mission, both yours and mine. Seeking wholeness is the mission of the church of Jesus Christ. We are called to nurture back to wholeness all those who struggle with trials, temptations, and addictions.

53 https://www.nytimes.com/2009/03/01/nyregion/01harvey.html

Did you know that addiction is the most untreated mental health condition in America today? Only one out of every ten persons with an addiction to alcohol and/or drugs receives any treatment at all. What if we could break this terrible cycle? What if the church could be open and honest? What if we told the truth, the whole truth, and nothing but the truth, so help us God? What if we could become vulnerable and practice the principles of Alcoholics Anonymous, Narcotics Anonymous, or any of the other twelve-step ministries?

Jesus said, "Do unto others as you would have them do unto you."

Maybe if we actually practiced what Jesus preached, more people would learn to fly, and fewer would fall flat on their faces.

⌒

The Distracted Life

BASED ON MATTHEW 22: 34-40

ARE YOU DISTRACTED? Does it sometimes feel as if you are being pulled in a million different directions by far too many demands? Does every item on your to-do list have the word urgent scribbled next to it? Do you hear voices, both real and imagined, telling you to *do this* and *do that* until finally you lose your focus and find yourself frazzled and worn out?

Distraction is a common problem in our culture today. We live in the hurried world of the Red Queen from Lewis Carroll's *Through the Looking-Glass:* "My dear, here we must run as fast as we can, just to stay in place. And if you wish to go anywhere you must run twice as fast as that."[54] We live distracted lives, don't we? We chase after many things: career, money, success, power, recognition, and security. We want it all, and as a result, we miss out on the most important part of our lives—meaningful relationships with others.

I learned this lesson long ago the hard way. I was a young up-and-coming associate pastor serving a large and prominent church with many assigned areas of ministry to oversee and

---

54   Lewis Carroll, *Alice's Adventures in Wonderland,* was first published in 1865. It has never been out of print.

develop. It was an all-consuming task, and I felt I had no time to breathe. My life was scheduled from early morning through late evening. One morning I leaped out of bed, frantic to get to the church on time for a critically important meeting. There was only one problem. It was my day to drop my three children off at three different schools in three different parts of the city.

As we dashed out the door and piled into the car, I realized it was trash pickup day. I ran back into the house, grabbed the trash bin, and dragged it to the curb. I jumped in the car again and slammed the door on the sleeve of my suit jacket, pulverizing three cuff buttons. Unfazed, I peeled out of the driveway and pulled into the nearest McDonald's drive-through, ordering three Egg McMuffins and three OJ's for my three children, and then sped away.

One by one, I dropped my daughters off at their respective elementary and junior high schools, finally screeching to a halt in front of my four-year-old son's pre-school. I calculated that I had exactly two minutes to get him out of the car and inside, allowing me four minutes to get to my meeting six blocks away on time. I was removing my son's seatbelt while badgering him to hurry up. Peter became flustered and accidentally dropped his cup of orange juice on the floorboard of the car.

It exploded like a bomb! The lid flew off, and the sticky juice went everywhere. It was all over the floorboard, the roof headliner, the windshield, my son, and me. My suit, starched white shirt, and silk tie were drenched. What happened next continues to haunt me to this day. In a rage, and without thinking, I slapped my four-year-old on his leg and screamed, "Look what you've done! You've made a mess." Of course, my remorse was instantaneous. I immediately pulled my son close to me, hugged him tightly, and begged, "O Peter, I am so sorry! Can you ever forgive me?"

Twenty-five years later, I don't remember a thing about that "critically important meeting" at the church, but I still recall the exact words my four-year-old son spoke to me in that moment. With tears welling up in his brown eyes, he looked at me and said, "It's OK, Dad. You're still my best friend."

What I learned that day: Don't be distracted by things that don't matter. Focus instead on what matters most.

> *Teacher, which commandment in the law is the greatest?*
> *Jesus said to him, "You shall love the Lord your God with all your heart, and with all your soul, and with all your mind."*
> *This is the greatest and first commandment.*
> *And a second is like it: "You shall love your neighbor as yourself."*
> *On these two commandments hang all the law and the prophets."*[55]

It is perhaps the most important question ever posed in human history. The Sadducees and the Pharisees are interrogating Jesus, asking him a series of questions, not for the sake of gleaning wisdom from the rabbi, but rather to destroy him. Jesus has captivated the hearts of the people, and his followers are multiplying rapidly. He is viewed as a threat to

---

55　Matthew 22: 36-40

the religious establishment who despise him. However, with each succeeding question and attempt to trip him up, Jesus rises above the fray and leaves his detractors speechless.

Now comes the final question: *"Jesus, what is the most important law? What is the law that stands above all other laws?"*[56] Surely, The Sadducees must have been thinking, Jesus will stumble on this one. After all, the Law of Moses includes 613 precepts—all from God—all holy. There's no way Jesus can provide an adequate answer. If he offers the standard response that all laws are equally holy, he will be asked to explain why he has broken a number of these laws himself, like *healing on the sabbath*[57] and *allowing his disciples to eat with defiled hands.*[58] On the other hand, if he names only one law like *thou shalt not kill* or *honor thy mother and thy father,* he will be relegating all other laws to second-class status. He will be labeled a heretic and destroyed.

Instead, Jesus quotes Deuteronomy 6:

Hear, O Israel. You shall love the Lord your God with all your heart, and with all your soul, and with all your might.[59]

This, of course, is the Shema. Every Jew, young and old, recites it every day. They carry this law in their hearts. The Shema is at the core of everything they hold near and dear.

Next, Jesus quotes an obscure text from Leviticus 19

---

56   Matthew 22:37
57   Matthew 12:13
58   Matthew 15:20
59   Deuteronomy 6:5

that is tucked between laws against mating different kinds of animals and weaving different kinds of fabric together:

You shall love your neighbor as yourself. Love God. Love neighbor. These two laws are one and the same ...[60]

Jesus tells the Pharisees and Sadducees—love God, love neighbor—two sides of the same coin—you can't have one without the other. The author of 1 John 4:20 sums it up this way: *How can we love a God we haven't seen, if we don't love a neighbor we have seen?*[61]

In a distracted world where we are continuously being pulled in different directions by a million conflicting demands, what if *love God, love neighbor*[62] could become our new mantra? What if our distracted attempts at getting ahead in the world could simply give way to loving God and loving others? What if, instead of striving for more and more, we instead gave more and more of ourselves to others?

What if, instead of driving our children to soccer practice, piano lessons, little league baseball, dance recitals, Tae Kwon Do demonstrations, and countless other activities that teach them to become as distracted as we are, we simply loved them, played with them, and prayed with them?

⌒

---

60   Leviticus 19:34
61   1 John 4:20
62   Matthew 22:37-39

Recently, I took my seven-year-old and four-year-old grandsons, Luke and Levi, out for frozen yogurt. They're growing up so fast, and there is so little time. So, I left the office early, picked them up at home, and drove them to the yogurt place in the shopping center. I handed each of them a large bowl and told them to get whatever they wanted. They began running amuck from dispenser to dispenser, filling their bowls with different flavors of yogurt: cotton candy, tutti-frutti, chocolate mocha, and blueberry. Next, they went for the toppings: chocolate chips, M & M's, Skittles, sunflower seeds, and gummy worms. It all seemed to me to be one big, distracted mess!

When we finally reached the cashier and placed their messy over-filled bowls on the scale, it groaned under the weight. I feared I might have to take out a second mortgage to pay for their creations. We sat down at a table, and I watched and listened as my grandsons giggled and talked and dropped more yogurt in their laps than in their mouths. At this stage of the game, I typically would have become distracted by their antics. I might've even called them down a time or two, or spit on a napkin and wiped their messy mouths, or told them to stop spinning round and round on their stools.

But I didn't. I didn't allow myself to become distracted. Instead, I just sat there and savored the moment.

⌒

A Little Child Shall Lead Them
BASED ON ISAIAH 11: 1-10

A shoot shall come forth from the stump of Jesse, and a branch shall grow out of his roots ... the wolf shall live with the lamb, the leopard shall lie down with the kid, the calf and the lion and the fatling together, and a little child shall lead them.

REMEMBER YOUR CHILDHOOD? Remember how it felt to be a kid? You knew no limits. You could go anywhere, do anything, be anyone you wanted to be. All you needed was a little faith. Remember your childhood fantasy adventures? Perhaps you swam the English Channel? Captured Sasquatch? Flew to the moon? I did all of these things and more!

Think about the special powers or gifts you possessed as a child: The ability to fly. The ability to swim underwater for hours on end without ever resurfacing. The gift of x-ray vision. If you were raised in a Christian home, perhaps you even claimed the gifts of the Holy Spirit like wisdom, knowledge, or prophecy.

As a boy, I was blessed with three distinct gifts. First, I had the gift of faith. I never ever doubted God, not even for a moment. I always believed. Second, I had the gift of hope.

I've always been an optimist at heart. Finally, I had a green thumb. I could make anything grow: watermelon seeds, sweet potato vines, even avocado pits. I would take an avocado pit, impale it with toothpicks, place it in a glass of water, and produce a towering plant. When I was six years old, I grew a rose bush out of thin air. Well, almost. I took a cutting from a rose bush and stuck it in the ground with no water or fertilizer added—it grew! The old woman in whose yard I performed this wondrous feat declared me a miracle worker. The rose bush remained there and thrived for many years until the lady died, and the new owners of her home cut it to the ground.

How many of us have had the experience of feeling cut down—our childhood dreams and visions "dried up like a raisin in the sun," to quote poet Langston Hughes? Life can be tough, even for those who live privileged lives. All of us experience rough patches in life:

- The loss of a loved one,
- The end of a relationship—whether personal or in a public setting
- Betrayal—be it professional or private,
- A medical diagnosis
- The loss of faith in ourselves, humanity, or God

As we approach another anniversary of the Sandy Hook Elementary School massacre this month, I still can't wrap my head around a world where monstrous acts occur. I still grieve the loss of all those beautiful children. My grandson is the age those children would've been today had they survived. I still recall speaking out against gun violence in a sermon following the massacre and being severely chastised by church members who labeled me an anti-second amendment idiot. Maybe I am, but here are the facts (as of this writing in 2022): 2,307 mass shootings have shaken this nation since Sandy Hook. It has to stop.

I'm in solidarity with the late John Lennon, also a victim of gun violence, who once sang: "You may think I'm a dreamer, but I'm not the only one."[63] I dream of an end to wars and rumors of wars, children going to bed hungry, families being separated at the border, people unable to afford life-giving medications, and the growing chasm between the "haves" and the "have-nots." I pray for a time when the low places in the world will finally be lifted up.

Of course, low places have existed since the beginning of time. As beautiful as the world is, it is also filled with no small amount of danger, hurt, and pain. This is why the prophet Isaiah's words move me to tears every year in this season of Advent.

> *A shoot shall come forth from the stump of Jesse, and a branch shall grow out of his roots.*
> *the spirit of the lord shall rest on him, the spirit of wisdom and understanding,*
> *the spirit of counsel and might, the spirit of knowledge, and the fear of the lord.*

63   John Lennon, *Imagine*, Apple Records, 1971.

The wolf shall live with the lamb, the leopard shall lie down with the kid,
the calf and the lion and the fatling together, and a little child shall lead them.[64]

The prophet Isaiah offered a word of faith, hope, and love to God's people at a time when they were in a low place. Israel had been ruled for generations by greedy kings who were only in it for their own personal gain. As a result, in 722 BC, without leadership and in a weakened state, Israel fell to the Assyrians. Thousands were killed or taken captive, the economy went belly-up, and the land lay in ruins. A beautiful towering tree of a nation had become a dead stump.

Enter Isaiah, who was a forecaster of doom and gloom like most prophets of his day. In spite of Israel's defeat, Isaiah spoke a word of hope to the Israelites. "This dead stump of a nation is going to blossom," he tells them. "A branch will grow out of it. Peace and prosperity will reign. The wolf, lamb, calf, and lion will lie down together. You will be able to put down your weapons and study war no more. Oh! And a little child will lead this effort."

Of course, Isaiah didn't know the name of this child, but we do, don't we? Born in Bethlehem, raised in Nazareth, traveled throughout Galilee, crucified at Golgotha, resurrected in a tomb, and with us now in the presence and power of the Holy Spirit. Look around you! Do you see him? Do you

---

64   Isaiah 11: 1-2, 6

recognize this child? You should because we are the body of Christ and individually members of it, and any hope or joy we feel has been inspired by this child, Emmanuel, God with us.

Don't discount the power of children to pull us up from the low places of life! Recently, I read an op-ed out of South Africa captioned "The Rise of Child Activists." It highlights the stories of children from around the world who are making a positive difference—children like Greta Thunberg from Sweden, who has mobilized a global response to climate change, Joshua Wong and his crusade to bring democratic reform to Hong Kong, and several other children, including my own granddaughter, Vivian, and her crusade to produce a female version of the iconic Green Army Men toy figures, thereby reducing gender objectification in children's toys.

Like the prophet Isaiah, these children have found a way to cut through our false bravado and vain attempts to keep a stiff upper lip in challenging times. They remind us that what we want and need most in life is to be gathered up, held close, and loved. We need to be told that we are safe and all will be well. Beyond this world's ugliness, great beauty lies ahead. We want to believe that a sprig can emerge from the stump of Jesse, don't we? We want to believe that a broken relationship can be restored—that a smile can reappear on a long-grieving face—and that truth can triumph over lies. So, forget the shiny, expensive toys you typically lavish on your children at Christmas time. Give them something more important instead—give them faith, hope, and love.

⌒

Now, back to my gifted green thumb. When Karen and I were just a couple of kids in college, I presented her with a potted Ficus Benjamina or weeping fig tree for Valentine's Day. Believe it or not, we still have that tree today. For forty-five years now, I have watered, fertilized, and repotted that tree which now towers over me at nine feet tall. It has grown too large, and I have grown too old to handle it. So, what do you do with a living thing that has been with you for decades, through every wedding anniversary, every family death, and the birth of your children and grandchildren? Totally stumped, I recently put the question of what to do with the tree to my Facebook friends. And the #1 response:

Pass it on. Take cuttings from the tree, root them and give them to your children. Don't let the tree die!

Pass it on to the children.
Not a bad idea! Maybe we should do the same with our faith.

⌒

CHAPTER 7

Bonnie and Blithe, Good and Gay

Live Your Hallelujah!

BASED ON PSALM 100

All people that on earth do dwell,
sing to the Lord with cheerful voice:
serve him with joy, his praises tell,
come now before him and rejoice!

Know that the Lord is God indeed,
he formed us all without our aid;
we are the flock he loves to feed,
the sheep who by his hand are made. [65]

KNOWN AS THE "OLD HUNDREDTH," it is one of the best-loved and most frequently sung hymns in Christendom. A paraphrase of Psalm 100, the music dates to the sixteenth century and the lyrics to the seventeenth century. However, the arrangement we now sing in worship is pure Twentieth century. Famed English composer Ralph Vaughn Williams arranged it for the coronation of her majesty Queen Elizabeth II held in Westminster Abbey on June 2, 1953. The hymn was a real show-stopper!

---

65   "Old Hundredth," Louis Bourgeois, 1551.

Picture, if you will, this fairy tale event that took place almost seven decades ago. Imagine the pomp, pageantry, and joy surrounding it. It was the first-ever coronation broadcast to the world. Twenty million Brits, or two-thirds of the nation's population at that time, watched it on TV. Three million people lined the streets of London to see the Queen as she passed through the city in her carriage. More than 8,251 guests were packed inside Westminster Abbey, and 480 musicians provided music for the ceremony, including a full orchestra and the combined choirs of Westminster Abbey, St. Paul's Cathedral, and St. George's Windsor.

But the best part of the queen's coronation was the Old Hundredth. Ralph Vaughn Williams had suggested using a congregational hymn as a part of the ceremony, specifically his freshly written arrangement of the "Old Hundredth." It was a controversial idea. No coronation had ever included a congregational hymn before. Still, Elizabeth approved, and on that glorious day everyone sang, "All people that on earth do dwell, sing to the Lord with cheerful voice!"

The story of Elizabeth's coronation gives us a clue as to the type of occasion for which Psalm 100 was originally composed; a grand and glorious occasion of offering praise and thanksgiving to one who is being enthroned as monarch. Imagine faithful Jews from all over the ancient Near East making their way to Jerusalem. Together, they navigate the harsh countryside over treacherous roads in the stifling heat. Imagine the tension they felt while watching out for robbers and thieves as they drag behind them the animals they will sacrifice to God. Upon reaching their destination, the temple court, they find it jam-packed with thousands of pilgrims and the cacophony of their sacrificial animals. At the appointed time, a priest emerges from the temple, raises his arms, and begins to sing this hymn:

> *¹Make a joyful noise to the LORD, all the earth.*
>
> *²worship the LORD with gladness;*
> *come into God's presence with singing.*
>
> *³Know that the LORD is God.*
> *it is he that made us, and we are his;*
> *we are his people, and the sheep of God's pasture.⁶⁶*

Suddenly the massive gates behind the priest open, and the throng is invited inside. The celebration reaches a crescendo with all the stops pulled out. This is not the coronation of an ordinary monarch! This is the coronation of the living God!

> *⁴Enter his gates with thanksgiving,*
> *and his courts with praise.*
> *Give thanks to him, bless his name.*
>
> *⁵For the LORD is good;*
> *his steadfast love endures forever,*
> *and his faithfulness to all generations. ⁶⁷*

If you check out the superscription above this psalm in any translation of the Bible, you'll find the phrase "A song of

---

66   Psalm 100:1-3
67   Psalm 100:4-5

grateful praise to God." And this is precisely the point! You and I were created to praise God. It's the first thing we're called to do in the morning and the last thing we're called to do at night, not to mention the rest of the time in between.

⌒

The word "hallelujah" is derived from two Hebrew words: halal and YHWH. Halal means praise, and YHWH means Lord or God. So "Halal YHWH" means "praise the Lord" or "hallelujah." Can I get a "praise the Lord" from you? Can I get a "hallelujah!" right now? There now! Don't you feel better? Lighter? Less anxious? More hopeful? I know I do!

You and I were created for worship. We were created to sing hallelujah. But we don't. More often than not, we enter this beautiful temple (sanctuary), not with songs of thanksgiving, but rather obsessing about the shoes we wore or whether our hair is properly slicked down. As a result, we miss a possible encounter with the Living God.

Christian author Annie Dillard says we have no clue the power we invoke when we call on the name of God. Dillard says we're like children with chemistry sets mixing up a batch of explosives. Instead of sports coats and pretty dresses, we should wear crash helmets and hazmat suits to worship. Ushers should issue life preservers and signal flares instead of bulletins because "The sleeping God may wake someday and take offense or the living God may draw us out where we can never return."[68]

---

68   Annie Dillard, *Teaching a Stone to Talk,* 1982.

If you've ever had an encounter with the living God, then you know it, and you also know your life has been changed forever. By the way, our worship of God is not limited to the sanctuary. Worshiping God is about everything we say and do. It's about who we are as human beings. As a young man wrestling with God over a call to ordained ministry, I realized I needed to get in shape. So, one night I threw away my cigarettes, picked up a Bible, and began reading. I also started running—literally running—miles and miles a day. For me, worship is both spiritual and physical. I want to be the very best I can be for God.

Isn't this the reason Jesus entered the wilderness for forty days? To get himself fit. To prepare himself to live out his hallelujah for the glory of God. Living our hallelujah for God is not for the weak or faint-hearted. God calls us to let go and allow the divine to lead us.

This past weekend I found myself playing in the backyard with my six-year-old granddaughter Vivian. We ran and tagged each other and fought invisible dragons with imaginary swords. But then, out-of-the-blue, Vivian stopped and exclaimed, "Come on, Daddo! Let's dance!" We dance a lot together—wild and crazy dancing—gyrating and twisting—but we always do it inside the house, hidden away from the world. Outside in front of God and the neighbors, I felt threatened. I took Vivian's hand—and a deep breath—as we began dancing wildly, totally unbridled without fear or shame.

Despite what we may have been taught, God doesn't

demand perfection from us. God doesn't require us to have all of our ducks in a row. God just wants us. God wants a relationship with us. God wants our worship.

No human being has ever captured God's heart quite like King David, and I don't understand why. David had feet of clay. He could be a scoundrel, self-serving, vain, even immoral at times. But nobody could worship like David. David danced and gyrated before the Ark of the Covenant in his underwear as it was carried into the holy city of Jerusalem, and God loved David for it. Is it any wonder that a thousand years later, a renegade Jewish carpenter riding into Jerusalem on the back of a donkey would be hailed the son of David?

At the time of Queen Elizabeth's coronation on June 2, 1953, my mother was pregnant, one month pregnant, with me. I seriously doubt I leaped in my mother's womb that day as John the Baptist had leaped in the womb of his mother Elizabeth so long ago. Yet, even now, I still get a lump in my throat whenever I sing a majestic hymn of praise, or I recite the 100th Psalm, or I come to the table to give thanks for the One who is worthy of my worship.

⌒

From Me to We

LIFE CAN BE DOWNRIGHT OVERWHELMING, CAN'T IT? Competing sights, sounds, and signals bombard us at every turn. Personal and professional demands, not to mention endless to-do lists, stack up like cordwood, leaving us dazed and confused until, finally, we're compelled to bolt and run away to disconnect from the world. Of course, this is precisely what we need to do—disconnect—at least for a time.

We desperately need *margin* in our lives, don't we? We need that space that lies somewhere between the load we carry and the limits we can tolerate. We need time to ponder, pray, and regroup so that we can reconnect and be productive.

I did this very thing last weekend. I put some margin in my life. On a cool fall-like Saturday morning, I took a stroll along the Arkansas River trail, a seventeen-mile pathway that meanders along both sides of the Arkansas River through both Little Rock and North Little Rock. I planned the walk as intentional "me time," a time to be alone, clear my head, and commune with nature. It worked! The clear blue sky, the cool air, and the flowing river lifted my spirits and put a bounce in my step. I had planned a three-mile walk, but it turned into six miles instead.

Something else happened on the river trail. Instead of disconnecting from the world, I reconnected with it! Something about the walkers, runners, and bikers along the pathway energized me. I became inspired watching people—black, white, Asian, young, old, heavy, thin, those wearing spandex and others wearing cargo shorts—moms and dads pushing baby strollers and caregivers pushing their care-receivers in wheelchairs. It was the most diverse congregation I have had the opportunity to worship with in a long time, and with the sounds of Bruno Mars blasting in my earbuds, I felt like I was in a music video.

I found myself smiling and waving at total strangers. I leaned into strollers and kitschy-kitschy-cooed babies along the trail. I almost skipped as I moved along. If a flash mob had suddenly broken into dance, I would have eagerly joined them! I felt totally connected.

Seventeenth century poet and preacher John Donne was spot-on when he wrote: "No man [or woman] is an island, entire of itself; every man [woman] is a piece of the continent, a part of the main."[69] We were created to connect with God and one another. Sure, we are individuals with our own unique genetic makeup, fingerprints, and soul. Because of this, "me time" is critical, but so is "we time." Whether we realize it or not, we are connected to others from the moment we're

69 John Donne, "Meditation 17," *Devotions upon Emergent Occasions,* 1624.

conceived. Carried in our mother's womb for nine months, we are later fed, diapered, and nurtured within a larger community following our birth. Our connections continue to grow from here.

No matter how much we try to assert our independence, we human beings are interdependent. We cannot make this journey called life alone. The ever-popular American image of the Lone Ranger must, at some point, give way to St. Paul's image of the body of Christ. Look at Paul's words to the church at Ephesus:

> *I therefore, the prisoner in the Lord, beg you to lead a life worthy of the calling to which you have been called, with all humility and gentleness, with patience, bearing with one another in love, making every effort to maintain the unity of the spirit in the bond of peace. There is one body and one spirit, just as you were called to the one hope of your calling, one Lord, one faith, one baptism, one God and father of all, who is above all and through all and in all.*[70]

As in so many of his writings, Paul spends the first portion of his letter to the Ephesians outlining the doctrines of the church. He says that, in Jesus Christ, God has torn down the wall that separates Jews from Gentiles. All humanity now has access to God through Christ's death and resurrection. But then, in chapter four, Paul shifts from doctrine to moral application. As the body of Christ, how are we to live into this new reality of one Lord, one faith, and one baptism? Paul says we do

---

70   Ephesians 4: 1-6

it by practicing humility, gentleness, patience, and love—not cheap love—but a crucified love that bears all things, believes all things, hopes all things, and endures all things. Paul calls the Ephesians to nothing less than unity of the spirit.

Take note: Paul is talking here about unity, not uniformity. Unity is a spiritual bond. It's not something we do ourselves. It's a gift from the Holy Spirit. Uniformity, on the other hand, is the human Gestapo lockstep demand that everyone obey a rigid set of rules, beliefs, and behaviors. Unity has nothing to do with whether we're circumcised or not— whether we eat kosher food or not—unity is not about sharing the same socioeconomic status or political affiliation or even the same stances on issues like abortion, capital punishment, immigration, or human sexuality. Unity is about a God who loved the world so much that God gave God's only child for us, all of us. Unity comes when we see all people as children of God.

I went down to the Arkansas River Trail last weekend for some "me time," but instead, I found myself caught up in "we time" as I smiled, waved, high-fived, and kitschy-kitschy-cooed so many. I'm convinced that the "spiritual high" I felt derived from the diversity of those I met. I felt God's presence not only in those like me but also in those who were not like me at all. I reveled in greeting white babies, black babies, muscular bikers in spandex, chubby men in cargo shorts, experienced trailblazers, and those walking the trail for the first time. My faith has grown exponentially since my childhood days of singing, "Jesus loves me, this I know." Call me a radical, but after more than six decades of life experience, I've come to realize that God is so much bigger and so much more inclusive than I ever dreamed. So now, instead of singing "Jesus loves ME, this I know," I'm more inclined to croon, "Jesus loves US (all of us), this I know."

In chapter four, Paul pens these words:

But each of us was given grace according to the measure of Christ's gift. And the gifts he gave were that some would be apostles, some prophets, some evangelists, some pastors and teachers, to equip the saints for the work of ministry, for building up the body of Christ, until all of us come to the unity of the faith and of the knowledge of the son of God.[71]

Unity in diversity. One body, many parts. It takes a village. We Christ-followers find strength in inclusion. We always have, and we always will.

On the river trail last weekend, while listening to Bruno Mars and performing in my own personal Walter Mitty music video, I thought about that old Coca-Cola® commercial from the 1970s. You know, the one that assembled young people from all around the world and placed them on a mountain top in Italy. Each of them held a bottle of Coke® in their hand as they sang, "I'd like to teach the world to sing in perfect harmony." Remember? With its message of unity, it's still considered one of the best-loved and most influential ads in television history.

---

71 Ephesians 4: 7, 11-13

What you may not know is that the South African apartheid government at the time requested a version of the ad without the black actors before they would air it to their citizens. Coca-Cola® refused and immediately began pulling their investments in South Africa. This is what the church is all about—unity—remaining connected and inclusive, no matter what demands the world throws at us.

⟡

A Game of Catch

BASED ON LUKE 15: 11-32

ONE OF THE MOST MEANINGFUL GIFTS I ever received came unexpectedly on Father's Day 1995. I was busy opening a stack of presents my wife and daughters had given me when I noticed my eight-year-old son, Peter, standing quietly in the background. He was clutching a brown paper bag in his hand. "Peter has a Father's Day gift for you," Karen informed me. "Go ahead and give Dad his present," she encouraged our son. Timidly, Peter placed the odd-shaped package on my lap and waited for me to open it. "Look!" I exclaimed, reaching into the bag and pulling out the hidden treasure, "Look! It's a baseball glove!" I was puzzled. Why would my son give me, a forty-one-year-old man who doesn't play baseball, a baseball glove? As I pondered this unusual gift, my wife explained, "Peter picked it out himself. He thought maybe the two of you could play a game of catch sometime."

Suddenly I realized the significance of this particular Father's Day present. This glove was more than a gift. It was an invitation—an invitation to play a game of catch—an invitation to enter into a deeper relationship with my son. The glove was his invitation to connect with him. I was speechless. I hugged Peter and thanked him enthusiastically for the perfect Father's Day gift!

"Hey, Dad! Wanna play a game of catch?" How many fathers have been thrilled at the sound of these words? So, on a muggy Sunday afternoon in mid-June, I reluctantly dragged myself off the sofa and moved out into the summer sun to play a game of catch with a reincarnated version of Cy Young. It was not a pretty sight. My arm felt like lead, and my reflexes were sluggish. Let's face it, after more than four decades of wear and tear on the body, my energy level had diminished significantly. But Peter didn't mind. He insisted that I remain in the game.

⁓

Peter kept throwing fastballs at me, and I kept catching them. He gave it everything he had, while my responses more resembled a slow-motion replay. Before long, though, something extraordinary happened. We managed to create a kind of rhythm between the two of us—throw, catch, throw, catch. Suddenly we were playing like the pros. The connection had been made.

As my son and I stood on the front lawn, separated by a distance of 60 feet, there was much more than a baseball traveling between us. There was also a kind of understanding—a bond was being forged–one that transcended time and space. It was the bond of love.

Our relationship with God is similar to a game of catch. God has gifted us with everything we need to be connected to our Creator. God has given us life and the ability to know God deeply and intimately. God tosses the ball and invites us to toss it back: throw … catch, throw … catch. In exchange for God's love for us, God simply asks that we reciprocate by loving God and neighbor. God doesn't mind if we occasionally bobble the ball or even drop it occasionally. God simply asks that we pick it up and try again.

The gospel according to Luke tells a powerful story about a boy who grew weary of playing catch with his father—Luke 15:11-32. "Dad, I'm tired of playing catch with you. I've outgrown this two-bit backyard sandlot. I'm ready for the major leagues. I'm taking my glove, and I'm going to the city. I'm going to play baseball for the Yankees." So the boy leaves. He goes to the city, but he never makes it to first base. Instead, he ends up as a batboy for the team. He feels humiliated and defeated. Finally, the boy comes to his senses. "I know! I'll go home. Maybe Dad will forgive me. Maybe we can play a game of catch together."

With head hung low and baseball glove dangling at his side, the boy heads home. It is dark by the time he arrives in the old neighborhood. As he rounds the final corner, he is blinded by a dazzling light. His old backyard is awash with brilliance. As his eyes adjust to the stadium lights, the boy sees that every member of his family has gathered to welcome him home. Not surprisingly, at the center of the crowd, poised and ready to play a game of catch, is his father.

When will we ever learn what every eight-year-old ball player already knows? It is more blessed to play catch with the Father than be left standing in the batting cage alone.

⌒

The Curse Reversed

DID I TELL YOU THERE IS A CURSE associated with my given name? Didn't I? Well, the curse is real. However, even I didn't learn about it until I was already a grown man.

I was named for my granduncle, Britt Allen Walt, who died in 1929 at the tender age of seventeen. His obituary indicates that, prior to his death, he had been ill for an entire year following a leg injury that occurred at a county fair.

Likewise, my granduncle Britt was named for his uncle, my great-granduncle, Britt Allen Willeford, who died in 1914 at the age of twenty-five. He was found semiconscious in a Little Rock alleyway by a police officer and died hours later at the city hospital from acute Bright's disease.

Finally, my great-granduncle Britt and my granduncle Britt were named for their father and grandfather, my great-great-grandfather, Brittain Smith Willeford, who died December 2, 1891, at the age of forty-one.

It's not difficult to see a pattern emerging here, is it? Forty-one years. Twenty-five years. Seventeen years. With each succeeding generation, the "Britts" on our family tree seemed to be dying at an ever-younger age. So, my family made a unanimous decision to break the terrible curse. The next generation of our family would include no Britts. The name had become taboo.

However, after a generation without any Britts in the family, when I arrived on the scene, my mom decided to put the old family curse to a test. She named me Britt in honor of my dearly departed ancestors, and all seemed well. I passed the seventeen-year mark the last "Britt victim" had reached without a hitch.

Now, fast forward several years. When I was a newly-married twenty-year-old college student living on campus with my bride in a small manufactured home, I faced a crisis. I returned to our place between classes one day to find the door of our abode standing wide open and our newly-adopted cocker spaniel puppy Jazz cowering in the corner. I stepped inside and heard a strange noise coming from the back bedroom. Using my backpack as a potential weapon, I slowly made my way down the hallway, where I came face-to-face with a uniformed maintenance man from the university.

"What are you doing here?" I breathlessly asked him.

"I have a work order for this unit," he replied, "It says your heater is on the blink."

"I didn't call maintenance," I respond, "and neither did my wife. We left together for class this morning."

"Well, somebody called," he told me as he went about his business.

I called the maintenance office. "There's somebody here inside unit fifty working on our heater, and he's telling me that we called to make the appointment."

"That's right—took the call myself," the disembodied voice at the other end of the line told me.

"Who called?" I ask.

"I don't know. It was a woman's voice, sounded like she might've been elderly. She was concerned. She said there was a problem with the heater, and we should come right away."

"OK, well, maybe my wife called after all," I respond apologetically.

About this time, Karen walked through the door. "Did you call maintenance about the heater?" I ask her.

"No," she responded, "You know I don't know anything about heaters! Is something wrong?"

"I'm not sure," I said as I turned and walked back down the hallway to the maintenance man, who was awaiting the result of my call.

"Hey!" he exclaimed, holding up a piece of unidentifiable metal. "It's a good thing you called when you did. This valve is in terrible shape. It could've blown up at any moment! You and the missus could've been seriously injured or even killed!"

Now, I must tell you. I am not given to flights of fancy. It is quite possible the work order phoned in for heater repair that day was intended for unit forty and not unit fifty. It is also possible the person in the maintenance office who took the call was high on hallucinogenic drugs. Or perhaps the maintenance man who announced the heater valve was about to explode was prone to hyperbole. I don't know for sure.

All I know is that, when I was told the voice of the caller who had reported the heater problem sounded like that of an elderly woman, my late great-grandmother Ruth immediately came to mind. Ruth had been a pivotal figure during my childhood years. I spent hours on a porch swing with my great-grandmother as she told me story after story about our family. As a result, much of my love for storytelling originated with Ruth. Ironically, I was the last member of the family to visit my great-grandmother before she suffered a massive stroke and died at the age of seventy-nine in 1966.

Ruth was so much more than my great-grandmother. She was also the mother of *Britt,* who died at the age of seventeen. And she was the big sister of *Britt,* who died at the age of twenty-five in a Little Rock alleyway. And she was the daughter of *Britt,* who died at the age of forty-one when she was a five-year-old girl.

I like to believe that my great-grandmother came to my rescue on that fateful day almost fifty years ago. I like to think that, from her heavenly perch, she announced to anyone and everyone who would listen, "Enough is enough! First, it was my father! Then it was my brother! And finally, it was my own beloved son! It's not going to happen again, not with my great-grandson. This curse has officially been reversed!" And she followed it up with a call to the maintenance office on my college campus.

⌇⌐

If you have enjoyed this book, point your browser to:
www.parkhurstbrothers.com